THE LIVING WILL
SOURCE BOOK
With Forms

Phillip Williams

The P. Gaines Co.
P.O. Box 2253
Oak Park, IL 60303

Library of Congress Cataloging in Publication Data

Williams, Phil, 1946-
   The living will source book, with forms.

   1. Right to die--Law and legislation--
United States--States.   2. Right to die--
Law and legislation--United States--States--
Forms.   I. Title.
KF3827 .E87Z9587   1986   344.73'0419   86-14962
                                    347.304419
   ISBN 0-936284-22-6 (pbk.)

First Printing, August 1986

ACKNOWLEDGMENTS

We gratefully acknowledge the assistance of Amy Godinez, who designed the cover, Attorney Jean Whalen, who provided research aid, and Doug Carey, who dealt with many different production tasks and problems too numerous to mention.

DEDICATION

This book is dedicated to all those who have worked to make the process of dying a more humane and meaningful event.

TABLE OF CONTENTS

Chapter 1.
THE LIVING WILL

Definition, Origin, and Brief History

The Living Will is a signed, dated, and witnessed document which permits you to authorize in advance the withholding or withdrawal of artificial life-support measures in the event of your terminal illness or injury. The term, first coined by attorney Luis Kutner in the 1930s, is obviously not new, although it is only in the last few years that a majority of states have passed "natural death acts," further underscoring the legal right of individuals to make Living Wills. Bishop Fulton Sheen was the first person officially to execute Kutner's "testament permitting death" without heroic medical treatments; actor Errol Flynn was the second. In 1968, Concern for Dying, a New York educational council, became the first organization to produce and distribute Living Wills. Since that time, millions of copies have been placed in the hands of those wishing to make advance directives about their own dying.

Ethical Grounds in the Modern Medical Context

While "advances" in medical science have developed procedures to keep those dying alive indefinitely by artificial means, many ethical thinkers have expressed grave reservations about this development, noting the absurdity of always doing what is possible by means of state-of-the-art medical technology. To keep some bodily functions alive when there is no reasonable chance of an individual's restoration to a minimal form of health or to resuscitate a terminally ill patient against his or her express wishes is morally repugnant to many. Such an impersonal application of medical technology to sustain life at any cost not only violates the individual's legal right to consent to or refuse medical treatment (unless opposed by a compelling state interest), but also one's ethical right to choose death when the body is hopelessly ill, beyond recovery.

In the modern hospital context, many persons in the advanced stages of terminal illness are unconscious or otherwise seriously impaired when artificial life-prolonging procedures are applied. A Living Will document provides one means of advance expression of one's wishes concerning medical treatment while one is still capable of deciding for oneself. Many states also specifically recognize by law one's right to have a guardian make treatment decisions when one is no longer competent to do so oneself.

Personalized Instructions

In addition to a general declaration forbidding the artificial prolongation of the life of a terminally ill person, many states with natural death
laws permit personalized instructions, for example, that one's dying not be
prolonged by specifically listed medical procedures, such as artificial
respirators, cardiopulmonary resuscitation, intravenous or nasogastric tube
feeding, blood transfusions, amputation, dialysis, and so on. Another frequently included personal direction in a Living Will document is the making of
a gift of one's body parts for transplantation or other purposes under the
Uniform Anatomical Gift Act. If any of these "additions" conflict with current
state law, they may be disregarded by the attending physician, however.

The Food and Water Controversy

Turning off a respirator when a patient is in an irreversible coma and
following a patient's prior approval of a "do not resuscitate" order are
generally recognized as standard medical practice at present. Today, the main
ethical and legal battles are being fought over the controversial issue of
withholding food and water, artificially administered intravenously or by
nasogastic tubes. The American Medical Association's Ethical and Judicial
Council has recently approved a policy statement which affirms the ethical
right to withhold all means of life-prolonging treatment (including nutrition
and hydration) from patients who are brain dead. In the past, the great
obstacle to implementation of Living Wills frequently has been a form of
medical paternalism which simply refused to take patients' wishes regarding
medical treatment into account. Growing public awareness of and education
about patient rights, evidenced by the ground swell of new natural death
legislation in dozens of states, have been paralleled by the medical communi-
ty's increasingly affirmative recognition of patient autonomy. The AMA's
latest policy statement is a much more revolutionary step than that adopted by
the courts to date.

In the noted case of Karen Quinlan, although the respirator was eventually
turned off with court approval, Karen continued to breathe on her own; because
she was fed artificially, she lived on, comatose, for some ten years more, much
to the horror of her family. It is precisely this form of "living death" that
advocates of the Living Will concept wish to abolish. With some 10,000
comatose individuals in this country today who are being sustained by artificial feeding (often against the express wishes of their families), this issue
is taking on mounting urgency.

Since no clear-cut pattern regarding the definition of "medical treatment"
has emerged from the courts--some permitting the withdrawal of artificial
feeding, others prohibiting it--the final resolution of this issue is still to
be thrashed out. The AMA statement, while not legally binding, does bolster
the arguments of those who favor withholding artificially administered sustenance as well as other forms of life-prolonging medical treatment for the
terminally ill.

Most recently, a California appeals court in a case involving Elizabeth

Bouvia, a quadriplegic victim of cerebral palsy, ruled that a patient's legal right to refuse medical treatment extends to the rejection of a feeding tube. The California appeals court affirmed a patient's basic and fundamental right to refuse medical treatment, even though it leads to death. This decision may well mark a turning point in the courts' interpretation of the individual's right to die.

Patient and Physician Safeguards

The Living Will has medical, legal, and ethical dimensions. It involves patient directives concerning specific medical treatments. It is also a legal document which, in certain states, carries fines and imprisonment or other sanctions if its terms are not adhered to by the attending physician. Finally, its existence depends upon certain ethical principles regarding human rights, including the right to a quality of life which goes beyond merely physical duration and, in the absence of such quality, the right to die. The Living Will concept provides medical, legal, and ethical safeguards for both patient and doctor, allowing a patient with a terminal condition the right to die without artificially protracted suffering and prolonged dying, as well as protecting the physician and other medical personnel carrying out the patient's wishes from civil or criminal liability or charges of unprofessional conduct.

Legal Basis in Constitution and Common Law

To date, 36 states and the District of Columbia have passed legislation detailing the legal rights of individuals who execute Living Will documents. It is the opinion of civil libertarians that these rights, moreover, are guaranteed by the Constitution and by common law rulings, in the absence of specific Living Will legislation. In other words, the fundamental rights which these laws address are operable even in those states which have not passed legislation dealing with this particular issue. These include the constitutional guarantee of individual privacy and the common law right to personal self-determination. Persons living in states without specific living will legislation can still fill out a Living Will, as explained below.

Specific State Laws Governing the Execution of a Living Will

Since the laws of states with Living Will legislation vary considerably on specific issues and some are more limited in scope and application than others, this book includes point by point the legal statutes for each state, as well as an Appendix with the required or recommended Declaration or Directive which each state legislature has approved. For individuals residing in states without specific legislation in this area, a general Living Will form with instructions is also provided in Appendix B.

Executing Your Living Will: State-mandated Declaration vs. Generic Form

It is strongly recommended that individuals living in states with natural death laws also fill out the "generic" Living Will form in Appendix B in addition to the state-mandated Declaration. There are three main reasons for this suggested precaution. First, only three states at present honor Declarations executed in other states. In the event of illness or injury away from your own state of residence, you will have a better chance of protecting your rights as an out-of-state medical patient. Second, the Living Will in Appendix B includes a Durable Power of Attorney by which an individual can designate some other person as his legal guardian in questions concerning medical treatment. This simply represents one more safeguard that one's wishes will be respected in the event that, in the course of terminal illness or injury, one becomes unconscious or mentally disabled and can no longer direct one's own treatment. Third, some states do not allow personalized instructions to be added to the Declaration; others permit certain types of additions but specifically forbid others (such as the withholding of artificial feeding). In this respect, you can use the generic Living Will form as a supplementary or complementary document in conjunction with the state recommended or required Declaration. The advantages of and rationale for doing so will be discussed below.

Definition of Key Terms

Each state with Living Will legislation generally provides a definition of key terms used in its natural death laws. We have not repeated the particular definitions of these terms for each state, since the meaning in most cases is obvious from the context (if not, it is stated). The terms frequently defined in this fashion include "Attending physician," "Adult" (most often, someone at least 18 years of age), "Declaration" or "Directive" or "Terminal Care Document" (the Living Will document executed in accordance with the natural death laws of that state), "Hospital," "Terminal Condition," "Qualified Patient" (someone who has executed a Declaration and has been diagnosed to be in a terminal condition). One term, that used to designate the medical treatments that prolong dying, is of particular significance and concern. In Mississippi, it is called "life-prolonging mechanisms"; in Missouri, "death-prolonging procedures"; in Maryland, "life-sustaining procedure." Regardless of the terminology employed, it is important to note what this key term includes as well as excludes in each state's natural death legislation, which has a direct bearing on other specific, personalized directives you may wish to make. In general, life-sustaining procedures or mechanisms include any medical treatment, procedure, or intervention which uses mechanical or other artificial means to sustain, restore, or supplant a spontaneous vital function (a mechanical respirator, for example). Most states specifically exclude pain medication and other forms of "comfort care" (in other words, these types of treatment are to be continued after a Living Will document takes effect and other forms of treatment are withdrawn).

Personalized Directions in Conflict with State Law

The "grey area," as already pointed out, concerns the issue of the withholding or withdrawal of nutrition and hydration. Some state laws specifically exclude food and water from the definition of life-sustaining procedures. Therefore, you may continue to be fed artificially even if you are unconscious and in an irreversible coma, unless you request in writing that these forms of treatment be discontinued. Because the legal precedents in this area are still far from clear, your wishes may or may not be followed. By making your desires known in writing, however, you greatly increase the chances of implementation. Since a Living Will document filled out at present may not become operable until some distant point in the future, the state laws may at that time allow for the implementation of a patient's directive which requests the withholding of food and water. Even if the present laws which, in many cases, explicitly forbid the withholding of sustenance continue in effect, your directives may be considered as advisory by your physician and may be legally implementable under certain circumstances. We have indicated in chapter 2 if a state's laws explicitly exclude nutrition and hydration from the category of life-sustaining procedures. If so, you must specify food and water, artificially administered, as other forms of treatment to be stopped during the dying process, if, in fact, it is your desire to do so, either by adding personalized instructions to the state Declaration, if allowable, or by including a directive to this effect in the supplemental Living Will form in Appendix B (or both). Ideally, all states will eventually follow the example of Tennessee, which legislatively distinguishes between artificial feeding (which may be discontinued in the event of a terminal condition) and normal feeding (which may not be withheld).

Overview of State Laws

A brief overview of some of the many variables in Living Will legislation from state to state provides an excellent introduction to the issues at stake. A little more than half the states with natural death laws at present specify that a Living Will document is invalid during pregnancy. In many states, only one attending physician is required to diagnose a patient's condition as terminal. In Maryland, two physicians must so certify, and in Mississippi the diagnosis of a terminal condition by the attending physician must be verified by two other physicians (three physicians in total must concur, in other words).

Some states, such as Maryland and Indiana, not only legally provide for a Declaration authorizing the withholding or withdrawal of life-sustaining procedures but also allow for a Declaration directing the initiation or continuation of life-sustaining procedures.

Missouri's law enjoins that "communication regarding treatment decisions among patients, the families, and physicians is encouraged." If this advice were universally followed, the various medical, legal, and ethical dilemmas that sometimes arise in the course of the implementation of a Living Will document would be resolvable in most cases.

In Virginia, Louisiana, Arizona, and several other states, the law outlines a nonjudicial procedure whereby another person may make a Declaration on behalf of comatose or incompetent patients who have no Declaration. Under Louisiana law, for example, other individuals, including a judicially appointed curator, spouse, adult child of the patient, the patient's parents, or the patient's sibling may make a Declaration on his behalf, provided he is comatose, incompetent, or physically or mentally incapable of communication and has been certified by two physicians as having a terminal and irreversible condition. Of course, there are judicial procedures available in other states which permit similar action on behalf of comatose or incompetent terminal patients without a Declaration.

About one-third of the states make legal provision for fines and imprisonment or other sanctions in the case of physicians who fail to adhere to the patient's rights set forth in its Living Will legislation. Some states, including Arizona and Texas, permit minors to make Declarations.

Mississippi raises the issue of transplants. According to Mississippi law, a physician participating in a decision to withdraw life-sustaining mechanisms from a patient at his wishes may not participate in transplanting the vital organs of the patient to another person.

All states require witnesses to the Declaration (normally, two witnesses, although South Carolina requires three). Many states exclude as witnesses persons related to the patient by blood or marriage, those entitled to a portion of the patient's estate as heirs or claimants, those responsible for the patient's health care costs, and employees or patients of the medical facility in which the patient is being treated.

Under Missouri law, a potential inheritor who acts contrary to the patient's wishes regarding the withholding or withdrawal of life-support mechanisms may lose the rights of inheritance to the extent such loss is provided for in the patient's last will and testament.

In California, Georgia, Idaho, Wisconsin, Delaware, and Oregon, the Declaration expires after a specified number of years and must be reexecuted to remain in effect. Almost all states provide for formal or informal means of revoking the Declaration.

In California, Georgia, Idaho, Oregon, and Texas, the state-legislated form of the Declaration must be followed exactly. Other states allow for personalized instructions. In three states (California, Idaho, and Oklahoma), the Declaration must be executed (or reexecuted) after the diagnosis of a terminal illness in order to be legally binding. Several states require the Declaration to be notarized, although it is advisable that all Living Will documents be notarized to shown the seriousness of one's intentions. Only a few states (Maine, Maryland, and Montana) specifically recognize Living Will documents executed out of state.

Clearly, the natural death laws of some states at present are much more backward and cumbersome to implement than others. Clarification and streamlining of these states' statutes should result in time.

"Significant Others" and Your Living Will

Once you have filled out a Living Will declaration, you should discuss it with your physician, attorney, clergyman, spouse, relatives, close friends, or others who may be involved in decisions related to your dying. You will want to provide a copy to your doctor for inclusion in your medical records and perhaps to other of the above-named individuals as well. If your doctor indicates that he is unwilling to comply with the tenets of your Living Will, you may wish to find another doctor more sympathetic to your concerns in this area. If you are naming someone else in the Durable Power of Attorney clause of the general Living Will form to make treatment decisions for you in the event of your incapacity, you will also want to discuss this matter with this designated "attorney-in-fact" (who, of course, does not need to be an attorney but may be anyone willing to serve in this capacity as your representative).

Living Will Registry

The Concern for Dying organization maintains a Living Will registry. In the event of an accident or sudden illness, a wallet card mini-will provided by this group will alert medical staff to contact the registry for a copy of your complete Living Will. The registry service is especially recommended for those without family members or close friends, although it will benefit anyone who decides to complete a Living Will document. Concern for Dying's staff will ensure that your document is filled out correctly, assign you a registry number, and keep a copy of your Living Will on file. If you or your representative acting on your behalf needs counseling or legal guidance in implementing your Living Will, one of their staff members will advise you. For details regarding these and other services pertaining to the Living Will, ranging from emotional support to legal counseling, contact

> Concern for Dying
> 250 West 57 Street
> New York, New York 10107
> Telephone (212) 246-6962

Chapter 2.
SPECIFIC STATE LAWS GOVERNING THE EXECUTION OF A LIVING WILL

This chapter consists of a point-by-point presentation of each state's natural death laws. All states with such legislation to date are covered in alphabetical order.

ALABAMA: NATURAL DEATH ACT (1981)

Legislative intent. The legislature finds that adult persons have the fundamental right to control the decisions relating to the rendering of their own medical care, including the decision to have life-sustaining procedures withheld or withdrawn in instances of a terminal condition. In order that the rights of patients may be respected even after they are no longer able to participate actively in decisions about themselves, the legislature hereby declares that the laws of this state shall recognize the right of an adult person to make a written declaration instructing his or her physician to withhold or withdraw life-sustaining procedures in the event of a terminal condition.

Execution of declaration. Any adult person may execute a declaration directing the withholding or withdrawal of life-sustaining procedures in a terminal condition. The declaration made pursuant to this act shall be: (1) In writing; (2) Signed by the person making the declaration, or by another person in the declarant's presence and by the declarant's expressed direction; (3) Dated; and (4) Signed in the presence of 2 or more witnesses at least 19 years of age.

Witnesses. Neither of the witnesses shall be the person who signed the declaration on behalf of and at the direction of the person making the declaration, related to the declarant by blood or marriage, entitled to any portion of the estate of the declarant according to the laws of intestate succession of this state or under any will of the declarant or codicil thereto, or directly financially responsible for declarant's medical care.

Pregnancy. The declaration of a qualified patient diagnosed as pregnant by the attending physician shall have no effect during the course of the qualified patient's pregnancy.

Notification of physician. It shall be the responsibility of declarant to provide for notification to his or her attending physician of the existence of the declaration. An attending physician who is so notified shall make the declaration, or a copy of the declaration, a part of the declarant's medical records.

Recommended form of declaration. See Appendix. The declaration shall be substantially in this form, but in addition may include other specific directions. Should any of the other specific directions be held to be invalid, such invalidity shall not affect other directions of the declaration which can be given effect without the invalid direction, and to this end the directions in the declaration are severable.

Definition of life-sustaining procedure; excluded treatments. Life-sustaining procedure shall not include the administration of medication or the performance of any medical procedure deemed necessary to provide comfort or care or to alleviate pain.

Revocation. A declaration may be revoked at any time by the declarant by any of the following methods: (1) By being obliterated, burnt, torn, or otherwise destroyed or defaced in a manner indicating intention to cancel; (2) By a written revocation of the declaration signed and dated by the declarant or person acting at the direction of the declarant ; or (3) By a verbal expression of the intent to revoke the declaration, in the presence of a witness 19 years of age or older who signs and dates a writing confirming that such expression of intent was made. Any verbal revocation shall become effective upon receipt by the attending physician of the above mentioned writing. The attending physician shall record in the patient's medical record the time, date, and place of when he or she received notification of the revocation. There shall be no criminal or civil liability on the part of any person for failure to act upon a revocation made pursuant to this section unless that person has actual knowledge of the revocation.

Certification and confirmation of a terminal condition. An attending physician who has been notified of the existence of a declaration executed under this act, without delay after the diagnosis of a terminal condition of the declarant, shall take the necessary steps to provide for written certification and confirmation of the declarant's terminal condition (diagnosis of 2 physicians, including attending physician, required), so that declarant may be deemed to be a qualified patient under this act.

Effectiveness of declaration. The desires of a qualified patient shall at all times supersede the effect of the declaration.

Presumption of validity. If the qualified patient is incompetent at the time of the decision to withhold or withdraw life-sustaining procedures, a declaration executed in accordance with this act is presumed to be valid. For the purpose of this act, a physician or medical care facility may presume in the absence of actual notice to the contrary that an individual who executed a declaration was of sound mind when it was executed. The fact of an individual's having executed a declaration shall not be considered as an indication of a declarant's mental incompetency. Age of itself shall not be a bar to a determination of competency.

Immunity. No physician, licensed health care professional, medical care facility, or employee thereof who in good faith and pursuant to reasonable medical standards causes or participates in the withholding or withdrawing of life-sustaining procedures from a qualified patient pursuant to a declaration made in accordance with this act shall, as a result thereof, be subject to criminal or civil liability, or be found to have committed an act of unprofessional conduct.

Refusal to comply; transfer. An attending physician who refuses to comply with the declaration of a qualified patient pursuant to this act shall not be liable for his refusal, but shall permit the qualified patient to be transferred to another physician.

Penalties. Any person who willfully conceals, cancels, defaces, obliterates, or damages the declaration of another without such declarant's consent or who falsifies or forges a revocation of the declaration of another shall be guilty of a Class A misdemeanor. Any person who falsifies or forges the declaration of another, or willfully conceals or withholds personal knowledge of the revocation of a declaration, with the intent to cause a withholding or withdrawal of life-sustaining procedures contrary to the wishes of the declarant, and thereby, because of such act, directly causes life-sustaining procedures to be withheld or withdrawn and death to be hastened, shall be guilty of a Class C felony.

Suicide. The withholding or withdrawal of life-sustaining procedures from a qualified patient in accordance with the provisions of this act shall not, for any purpose, constitute a suicide and shall not constitute assisting suicide.

Insurance. The making of a declaration pursuant to this act shall not affect in any manner the sale, procurement, or issuance of any policy of life insurance, nor shall it be deemed to modify the terms of an existing policy of life insurance. No policy of life insurance shall be legally impaired or invalidated in any manner by the withholding or withdrawal of life-sustaining procedures from an insured qualified patient, notwithstanding any term of the policy to the contrary.

Conditional execution of declaration. No physician, medical care facility, or other health care provider, and no health care service plan, health maintenance organization, insurer issuing disability insurance, self-insured employee welfare benefit plan, nonprofit medical service corporation, or mutual nonprofit hospital or hospital service corporation shall require any person to execute a declaration as a condition for being insured for, or receiving, health care services.

Provisions of act cumulative. Nothing in this act shall impair or supersede any legal right or legal responsibility which any person may have to effect the withholding or withdrawal of life-sustaining procedures in any lawful manner. In such respect the provisions of this act are cumulative.

Presumption of intent. This act shall create no presumption concerning the intention of an individual who has not executed a declaration to consent to the use or withholding of life-sustaining procedures in the event of a terminal condition.

Mercy killing. Nothing in this act shall be construed to condone, authorize, or approve mercy killing or to permit any affirmative or deliberate act or omission to end life other than to permit the natural process of dying as provided in this act.

ARIZONA: MEDICAL TREATMENT DECISION ACT (1985)

Execution of declaration. A person 18 years or more of age may execute a declaration directing the withholding or withdrawal of life-sustaining procedures in a terminal condition.

Witnesses. The declarant must sign the declaration in the presence of 2 subscribing witnesses who are not: (1) Related to the declarant by blood or marriage; (2) At the time of the declaration, entitled to any portion of the estate of the declarant under a will of the declarant or a codicil to a will then existing or by operation of law then existing; (3) Claimants against any portion of the estate of the declarant at the time of his decease or at the time of the execution of the declaration; (4) Directly financially responsible for the declarant's medical care.

Notification to physician. The declarant is responsible for providing notification to his attending physician of the existence of the declaration. An attending physician who is notified of the existence of a declaration shall make the declaration, or a copy of the declaration, a part of the declarant's medical records.

Recommended form of declaration. For suggested form of declaration, see Appendix. The declaration shall be substantially in this form but may include other specific directions. If any of the other specific directions is held invalid, the invalidity does not affect other directions of the declaration which can be given effect without the invalid direction.

Definition of life-sustaining procedure; excluded treatments. "Life-sustaining procedure" does not include the administration of medication, food or fluids, or the performance of a medical procedure deemed necessary to provide comfort care.

Revocation of declaration. The declarant may revoke a declaration at any time without regard to his mental state or capacity by any of the following methods: (1) Cancellation, defacement, obliteration, burning, tearing, or other means of destruction by the declarant or by some person in his presence and by his direction; (2) A written revocation of the declarant expressing his intent to revoke, which is signed and dated by the declarant; (3) A verbal expression by the declarant of his intent to revoke the declaration.

Notification of revocation. Upon revoking a declaration, the declarant shall give notice to any physician who has been given notice of the declaration. The physician shall record in the patient's medical records the time and date when he received notification of the revocation. A verbal revocation becomes effective on communication to the attending physician by the declarant or by a person who is reasonably believed to be acting on behalf of the declarant. The attending physician shall record in the patient's medical record the time, date, and place of the revocation and the time, date, and place, if different, that he received notification of the revocation.

Physician's responsibility for written certification. An attending physician who is notified of the existence of a declaration executed as provided in this act shall, without delay after the diagnosis of a terminal condition of the declarant, take the necessary steps to provide for written certification and confirmation of the declarant's terminal condition so that the declarant may be deemed to be a qualified patient. ("Qualified patient" means a patient, 18 years or more of age, who executes a declaration as provided in this act and who is diagnosed and certified in writing to be afflicted with a terminal condition by 2 physicians who personally examined the patient, one of whom is the attending physician.)

Transfer. An attending physician who fails to comply with the above. section is deemed to have refused to comply with the declaration and shall make reasonable efforts to transfer the qualified patient or not hinder the transfer of that patient to another physician who will effectuate the declaration of the qualified patient.

Effect of declaration. The desires of a qualified patient who has capacity supersede the effect of a declaration.

Presumption of validity. If the qualified patient lacks capacity at the time of the decision to withhold or withdraw life-sustaining procedures, a declaration executed in accordance with this act is presumed to be valid. For the purpose of this act, a physician or health care institution may presume, in the absence of actual notice to the contrary, that a person who executed a declaration was of sound mind when it was executed. The fact that a person executed a declaration shall not be considered as an indication of a declarant's mental capacity. Age of itself is not a bar to a determination of capacity.

Immunity. No physician, health care institution, or licensed health professional who relies in good faith upon a declaration shall be subject to civil or criminal liability or be deemed guilty of unprofessional conduct for withholding or withdrawing life-sustaining procedures from a qualified patient pursuant to a declaration unless that person has actual notice of the revocation of the declaration.

Pregnancy. The declaration of a qualified patient known to the attending physician to be pregnant shall be given no force or effect as long as the fetus could develop to the point of live birth with continued application of life-sustaining procedures.

Guardian's responsibility. If a guardian is appointed for a person who has previously executed a declaration pursuant to this act, he shall: (1) Observe and honor any declaration or written or verbal revocation of a declaration made pursuant to this act; (2) Notify an attending physician of the existence of the declaration and its terms; (3) Verify any indication of revocation by the declarant made to the guardian by a person who claims to be acting on behalf of the declarant; (4) Upon receiving notice from a physician of written certification of a terminal condition, exercise his powers in a manner consistent with the declaration.

Insurance. The making of a declaration as provided in this act does not affect in any manner the sale, procurement, or issuance of any policy of life insurance, nor is it deemed to modify the terms of an existing policy of life insurance. A policy of life insurance is not legally impaired or invalidated in any manner by the withholding or withdrawal of life-sustaining procedures from an insured qualified patient, notwithstanding any term of the policy.

Conditional execution of declaration. A physician, a health care institution, any other health care provider, a health care service plan, an insurer issuing disability insurance, a self-insured employee welfare benefit plan, or a nonprofit hospital plan may not require a person to execute a declaration as a condition for being insured for or receiving health care services.

Suicide. The withholding or withdrawal of life-sustaining procedures from a qualified patient in accordance with this act does not, for any purpose, constitute a suicide.

Mercy killing. Nothing in this act shall be construed to condone, authorize, or approve mercy killing or euthanasia or to permit any affirmative or deliberate act or omission to end life, other than to permit the natural process of dying.

Penalties. A person who willfully conceals, cancels, defaces, obliterates or damages the declaration of another without the declarant's consent or who falsifies or forges a revocation of the declaration of another is civilly liable to any person damaged. A person who falsifies or forges the declaration of another, or knowingly conceals or withholds personal knowledge of a revocation, with the intent to cause a withholding or withdrawal of life-sustaining procedures contrary to the wishes of the declarant and, because of such act, directly causes life-sustaining procedures to be withheld or withdrawn and death to be hastened is guilty of a class 1 felony.

ARKANSAS: DEATH WITH DIGNITY ACT (1977)

Right to die with dignity or to have life prolonged. Every person shall have the right to die with dignity and to refuse and deny the use or application by any person of artificial, extraordinary, extreme, or radical medical or surgical means or procedures calculated to prolong his life. Alternatively, every person shall have the right to request that such extraordinary means be utilized to prolong life to the extent possible.

Written request. Any person, with the same formalities as are required by the laws of this state for the execution of a will, may execute a document exercising such right and refusing and denying the use or application by any person of artificial, extraordinary, extreme, or radical medical or surgical means or procedures calculated to prolong his life. In the alternative, any person may request in writing that all means be utilized to prolong life.

Who may execute written request for another. If any person is a minor or an adult who is physically or mentally unable to execute or is otherwise incapacitated from executing either document, it may be executed in the same form on his behalf: (a) By either parent of the minor; (b) By his spouse; (c) If his spouse is unwilling or unable to act, by his child aged 18 or over; (d) If he has more than 1 child aged 18 or over, by a majority of such children; (e) If he has no spouse or child aged 18 or over, by either of his parents; (f) If he has no parent living, by his nearest living relative; or (g) If he is mentally incompetent, by his legally appointed guardian. Provided, that a form executed in compliance with this section must contain a signed statement by 2 physicians that extraordinary means would have to be utilized to prolong life.

Form of document. None specified or recommended in the Arkansas statutes. It is suggested that the Living Will form in Appendix B be filled out by Arkansas residents.

No liability for actions in accordance with request. Any person, hospital, or other medical institution which acts or refrains from acting in reliance on and in compliance with such document shall be immune from liability otherwise arising out of such failure to use or apply artificial, extraordinary, extreme, or radical medical or surgical means or procedures calculated to prolong such person's life.

CALIFORNIA: NATURAL DEATH ACT (1976)

Legislative findings and declaration. The Legislature finds that adult persons have the fundamental right to control the decisions relating to the rendering of their own medical care, including the decision to have life-sustaining procedures withheld or withdrawn in instances of a terminal condition. The Legislature further finds that modern medical technology has made possible the artificial prolongation of human life beyond natural limits. The Legislature further finds that, in the interest of protecting individual autonomy, such prolongation of life for persons with a terminal condition may cause loss of patient dignity and unnecessary pain and suffering, while providing nothing medically necessary or beneficial to the patient. The Legislature further finds that there exists considerable uncertainty in the medical and legal professions as to the legality of terminating the use or application of life-sustaining procedures where the patient has voluntarily and in sound mind evidenced a desire that such procedures be withheld or withdrawn. In recognition of the dignity and privacy which patients have a right to expect, the Legislature hereby declares that the laws of the State of California shall recognize the right of an adult person to make a written directive instructing his physician to withhold or withdraw life-sustaining procedures in the event of a terminal condition.

Directive to withhold or withdraw life-sustaining procedures. Any adult person may execute a directive directing the withholding or withdrawal of life-sustaining procedures in a terminal condition, as diagnosed and certified in writing by 2 physicians who have personally examined the patient, one of whom shall be the attending physician. The directive shall be signed by the declarant in the presence of 2 witnesses.

Qualifications of witnesses. Neither witness shall be related to the declarant by blood or marriage, nor entitled to any portion of the estate of the declarant upon his decease under any will of the declarant or codicil thereto then existing or, at the time of the directive, by operation of law then existing. In addition, a witness to a directive shall not be the attending physician, an employee of the attending physician or a health facility in which the declarant is a patient, or any person who has a claim against any portion of the estate of the declarant upon his decease at the time of the execution of the directive.

Medical records. The directive, or a copy of the directive, shall be made part of the patient's medical records.

Required form of directive. See Appendix. The directive must be in exactly this form.

Definition of life-sustaining procedure; excluded treatments. "Life-sustaining procedure" shall not include the administration of medication or the performance of any medical procedure deemed necessary to alleviate pain.

Patient in skilled nursing facility; witnesses. A directive shall have no force or effect if the declarant is a patient in a skilled nursing facility as defined in subdivision (c) of Section 1250 at the time the directive is executed unless 1 of the 2 witnesses to the directive is a patient advocate or ombudsman as may be designated by the State Department of Aging for this purpose pursuant to any other applicable provision of law. The patient advocate or ombudsman shall have the same qualifications as a witness as specified in the section above titled "Qualifications of Witnesses." The intent of this section is to recognize that some patients in skilled nursing facilities may be so insulated from a voluntary decisionmaking role, by virtue of the custodial nature of their care, as to require special assurance that they are capable of willfully and voluntarily executing a directive.

Revocation of directive. A directive may be revoked at any time by the declarant, without regard to his mental state or competency, by any of the following methods: (1) By being canceled, defaced, obliterated, or burnt, torn, or otherwise destroyed by the declarant or by some person in his presence and by his direction. (2) By a written revocation of the declarant expressing his intent to revoke, signed and dated by the declarant. Such revocation shall become effective upon communication to the attending physician by the declarant or by a person acting on behalf of the declarant. The attending physician shall record in the patient's record the time and date when he received notification of the written revocation. (3) By a verbal expression by the declarant of his intent to revoke the directive. Such revocation shall become effective only upon communication to the attending physician by the declarant or by a person acting on behalf of the declarant. The attending physician shall record in the patient's medical record the time, date, and place of the revocation and the time, date, and place, if different, of when he received notification of the revocation. There shall be no criminal or civil liability on the part of any person for failure to act upon a revocation made pursuant to this section unless that person has actual knowledge of the revocation.

Duration of directive; reexecution. A directive shall be effective for 5 years from the date of execution thereof unless sooner revoked in a manner prescribed in the section above. Nothing in this act shall be construed to prevent a declarant from reexecuting a directive at any time in accordance with the formalities of this act, including reexecution subsequent to a diagnosis of a terminal condition. If the declarant has executed more than 1 directive, such time shall be determined from the date of execution of the last directive known to the attending physician. If the declarant becomes comatose or is rendered incapable of communicating with the attending physician, the directive shall remain in effect for the duration of the comatose condition or until such time as the declarant's condition renders him or her able to communicate with the attending physician.

Civil or criminal liability or unprofessional conduct. No physician or health facility which, acting in accordance with the requirements of this act, causes the withholding or withdrawal of life-sustaining procedures from a qualified patient, shall be subject to civil liability therefrom. No licensed health professional, acting under the direction of a physician, who partici-pates in the withholding or withdrawal of life-sustaining procedures in accordance with the provisions of this act, shall be subject to any civil liability. No physician, or licensed health professional acting under the direction of a physician, who participates in the withholding or withdrawal of life-sustaining procedures in accordance with the provisions of this act shall be guilty of any criminal act or of unprofessional conduct.

Implementation of directive by physician. (a) Prior to effecting a withholding or withdrawal of life-sustaining procedures from a qualified patient (that is, a patient certified to have a terminal condition) pursuant to the directive, the attending physician shall determine that the directive complies with this act, and, if the patient is mentally competent, that the directive and all steps proposed by the attending physician to be undertaken are in accord with the desires of the qualified patient. (b) If the declarant was a qualified patient at least 14 days prior to executing or reexecuting the directive, the directive shall be conclusively presumed, unless revoked, to be the directions of the patient regarding the withholding or withdrawal of life-sustaining procedures. No physician, and no licensed health professional acting under the direction of a physician, shall be criminally or civilly liable for failing to effectuate the directive of the qualified patient pursuant to this subdivision. A failure by a physician to effectuate the directive of a qualified patient pursuant to this division shall constitute unprofessional conduct if the physician refuses to make the necessary arrangements, or fails to take the necessary steps, to effect the transfer of the qualified patient to another physician who will effectuate the directive of the qualified patient. (c) If the declarant becomes a qualified patient subsequent to executing the directive, and has not subsequently reexecuted the directive, the attending physician may give weight to the directive as evidence of the patient's directions regarding the withholding or withdrawal of life-sustaining procedures and may consider other factors, such as information from the affected family or the nature of the patient's illness, injury, or disease, in determining whether the totality of circumstances known to the attending physician justify effectuating the directive. No physician, and no licensed health professional acting under the direction of a physician, shall be criminally or civilly liable for failing to effectuate the directive of the qualified patient pursuant to this subdivision. (In other words, the directive is only legally enforceable under California law if it is executed or reexecuted 14 days or more _after_ the diagnosis of a terminal condition; otherwise, it is only considered advisory of the patient's wishes.)

Suicide. The withholding or withdrawal of life-sustaining procedures from a qualified patient in accordance with the provisions of this act shall not, for any purpose, constitute a suicide.

Insurance. The making of a directive pursuant to this act shall not restrict, inhibit, or impair in any manner the sale, procurement, or issuance of any policy of life insurance, nor shall it be deemed to modify the terms of an existing policy of life insurance. No policy of life insurance shall be legally impaired or invalidated in any manner by the withholding or withdrawal of life-sustaining procedures from an insured qualified patient, notwithstanding any term of the policy to the contrary.

Conditional execution of directive. No physician, health facility, or other health provider, and no health care service plan, insurer issuing disability insurance, self-insured employee welfare benefit plan, or nonprofit hospital service plan, shall require any person to execute a directive as a condition for being insured for, or receiving, health care services.

Provisions of act cumulative. Nothing in this act shall impair or supersede any legal right or legal responsibility which any person may have to effect the withholding or withdrawal of life-sustaining procedures in any lawful manner. In such respect the provisions of this act are cumulative.

Penalties. Any person who willfully conceals, cancels, defaces, obliterates, or damages the directive of another without such declarant's consent shall be guilty of a misdemeanor. Any person who, except where justified or excused by law, falsifies or forges the directive of another, or willfully conceals or withholds personal knowledge of a revocation as provided in this act, with the intent to cause a withholding or withdrawal of life-sustaining procedures contrary to the wishes of the declarant, and thereby, because of any such act, directly causes life-sustaining procedures to be withheld or withdrawn and death to thereby be hastened, shall be subject to prosecution for unlawful homicide as provided in Chapter 1 (commencing with Section 187) of

Title 8 of Part 1 of the Penal Code.

Mercy killing. Nothing in this act shall be construed to condone, authorize, or approve mercy killing, or to permit any affirmative or deliberate act or omission to end life other than to permit the natural process of dying as provided in this act.

COLORADO: MEDICAL TREATMENT DECISION ACT (1985)

Legislative declaration. The general assembly hereby finds, determines, and declares that: (a) Colorado law has traditionally recognized the right of a competent adult to accept or reject medical or surgical treatment affecting his person; (b) Recent advances in medical science have made it possible to prolong dying through the use of artificial, extraordinary, extreme, or radical medical or surgical procedures; (c) The use of such medical or surgical procedures increasingly involves patients who are unconscious or otherwise incompetent to accept or reject medical or surgical treatment affecting their persons; (d) The traditional right to accept or reject medical or surgical treatment should be available to an adult while he is competent, notwithstanding the fact that such medical or surgical treatment may be offered or applied when he is suffering from a terminal condition and is either unconscious or otherwise incompetent to decide whether such medical or surgical treatment should be accepted or rejected; (e) This article affirms the traditional right to accept or reject medical or surgical treatment affecting one's person, and creates a procedure by which a competent adult may make such decisions in advance, before he becomes unconscious or otherwise incompetent to do so; (f) It is the legislative intent that nothing in this act shall have the effect of modifying or changing currently practiced medical ethics or protocol with respect to any patient in the absence of a declaration; (g) It is the legislative intent that nothing in this act shall require any person to execute a declaration.

Execution of declaration. Any competent adult at least 18 years of age may execute a declaration directing that life-sustaining procedures be withheld or withdrawn if, at some future time, he is in a terminal condition and either unconscious or otherwise incompetent to decide whether any medical procedure or intervention should be accepted or rejected. A declaration executed before 2 witnesses by any competent adult shall be legally effective for the purposes of this act.

Notification of physician. It shall be the responsibility of the declarant or someone acting for him to submit the declaration to the attending physician for entry in the declarant's medical record.

Pregnancy. In the case of a declaration of a qualified patient known to the attending physician to be pregnant, a medical evaluation shall be made as to whether the fetus is viable and could with a reasonable degree of medical certainty develop to live birth with continued application of life-sustaining procedures. If such is the case, the declaration shall be given no force or effect.

Inability of declarant to sign. In the event the declarant is physically unable to sign the declaration, it may be signed by some other person in the declarant's presence and at his direction. Such other person may not be: (a) The attending physician or any other physician; or (b) An employee of the attending physician or health care facility in which the declarant is a patient; or (c) A person who has a claim against any portion of the estate of the declarant at his death at the time the declaration is signed; or (d) A person who knows or believes he is entitled to any portion of the estate of the declarant upon his death either as a beneficiary of a will in existence at the time the declaration is signed or as an heir at law.

Witnesses. The declaration shall be signed by the declarant in the presence of 2 witnesses. Said witnesses shall not include any person specified in subsections (a) through (d) of the above section, titled "Inability of Declarant to Sign." If the declarant is a patient or resident of a health care facility, the witnesses shall not be patients of that facility.

Recommended form of declaration. For the suggested form which the declaration may, but does not have to, follow, see Appendix (form required to be notarized).

Withdrawal of life-sustaining procedures. In the event an attending physician is presented with an unrevoked declaration executed by a declarant whom the physician believes has a terminal condition, the attending physician shall cause the declarant to be examined by 1 other physician. If both physicians find that the declarant has a terminal condition, they shall certify such fact in writing and enter such in the qualified patient's medical record of the hospital in which the withholding or withdrawal of life-sustaining procedures may occur, together with a copy of the declaration. Provided the attending physician has actual knowledge of the whereabouts of the qualified patient's spouse, any of his adult children, a parent, or attorney-in-fact under a durable power of attorney, the attending physician shall immediately make a reasonable effort to notify at least 1 of said persons, in the order named, that a certificate of terminal condition has been signed. If no action to challenge the validity of a declaration has been filed within 48 consecutive hours after the certification is made by the physicians, the attending physician shall then withdraw or withhold all life-sustaining procedures pursuant to the terms of the declaration.

Determination of validity. Any person who is the parent, adult child, spouse, or attorney-in-fact under a durable power of attorney of the qualified patient may challenge the validity of a declaration in the appropriate court of the county in which the qualified patient is located. Upon the filing of a petition to challenge the validity of a declaration and notification to the attending physician, a temporary restraining order shall be issued until a final determination as to validity is made. In proceedings pursuant to this section, the court shall appoint a guardian ad litem for the qualified patient, and the guardian ad litem shall take such action as he deems necessary and prudent in the best interest of the qualified patient and shall present to the court a report of his actions, findings, conclusions, and recommendations. Unless the court for good cause shown provides for a different method or time of notice, the petitioner, at least 5 days prior to the hearing, shall cause notice of the time and place of hearing to be given as follows: (a) To the qualified patient's guardian or conservator, if any, and the court-appointed guardian ad litem; and (b) To the qualified patient's spouse, if the identity and whereabouts of the spouse are known, to the petitioner, or otherwise to an adult child or parent of the qualified patient. Notice as required in this paragraph shall be made in accordance with the Colorado rules of civil procedure. The court may require such evidence, including independent medical evidence, as it deems necessary. Upon a determination of the validity of the declaration, the court shall enter any appropriate order.

Revocation. A declaration may be revoked by the declarant orally, in writing, or by burning, tearing, cancelling, obliterating, or destroying said declaration.

Liability. With respect to any declaration which appears on its face to have been executed in accordance with the requirements of this act: (a) Any physician may act in compliance with such declaration in the absence of actual notice of revocation, fraud, misrepresentation, or improper execution; (b) No physician signing a certificate of terminal condition or withholding or withdrawing life-sustaining procedures in compliance with a declaration shall be subject to civil liability, criminal penalty, or licensing sanctions therefor; (c) No hospital or person acting under the direction of a physician and participating in the withholding or withdrawal of life-sustaining procedures in compliance with a declaration shall be subject to civil liability, criminal penalty, or licensing sanctions therefor.

Suicide or homicide. The withholding or withdrawal of life-sustaining procedures from a qualified patient pursuant to this act shall not, for any purpose, constitute a suicide or homicide.

Insurance. The existence of a declaration shall not affect, impair, or modify any contract of life insurance or annuity or be the basis for any delay in issuing or refusing to issue an annuity or policy of life insurance or any increase of the premium therefor.

Conditional execution of declaration. No insurer or provider of health care shall require any person to execute a declaration as a condition of being insured for or receiving health care services; nor shall the failure to execute a declaration be the basis for any increased or additional premium for a contract or policy for medical or health insurance.

Application of act; presumption of intent. Nothing in this act shall be construed as altering or amending the standards of the practice of medicine or establishing any presumption in the absence of a valid declaration.

Excluded treatments under the definition of life-sustaining procedure. "Life-sustaining procedure" shall not include any medical procedure or intervention to nourish the qualified patient or considered necessary by the attending physician to provide comfort or alleviate pain.

Mercy killing. Nothing in this act shall be construed to condone, authorize, or approve euthanasia or mercy killing, nor to permit any affirmative or deliberate act or omission to end life, except to permit natural death as provided in this act.

Conflict of provisions. In the event of any conflict between the provisions of this act, or a declaration executed under this act, and the provisions of section 15-14-501, the provisions of this act and the declaration shall prevail.

Penalties. Any person who willfully conceals, defaces, damages, or destroys a declaration of another, without the knowledge and consent of the declarant, commits a class 1 misdemeanor and shall be punished as provided in section 18-1-106, C.R.S. Any person who falsifies or forges a declaration of another commits a class 4 felony and shall be punished as provided in section 18-1-105, C.R.S. Any person who falsifies or forges a declaration of another, and the terms of the declaration are carried out, resulting in the death of the purported declarant, commits a class 2 felony and shall be punished as provided in section 18-1-105, C.R.S. Any person who willfully withholds information concerning the revocation of the declaration of another commits a class 1 misdemeanor and shall be punished as provided in section 18-1-106, C.R.S.

Transfer; penalty. An attending physician who refuses to comply with the terms of a declaration valid on its face shall transfer the care of the declarant to another physician who is willing to comply with the declaration. Refusal of an attending physician to comply with a declaration and failure to transfer the care of the declarant to another physician shall constitute unprofessional conduct as defined in section 12-36-117, C.R.S.

CONNECTICUT: AN ACT CONCERNING DEATH WITH DIGNITY (1985)

General provisions. Any physician licensed under Chapter 370 of the general statutes of Connecticut or any licensed medical facility which removes or causes the removal of a life-support system of an incompetent patient shall not be liable for damages in any civil action or subject to prosecution in any criminal proceeding for such removal, provided (1) The decision to remove such life-support system is based on the best medical judgment of the attending physician; (2) The attending physician deems the patient to be in a terminal condition; (3) The attending physician has obtained the informed consent of the next of kin, if known, or legal guardian, if any, of the patient prior to removal; and (4) the attending physician has considered the patient's wishes as expressed by the patient directly, through his next of kin or legal guardian, or in the form of a document executed in accordance with this act, if any such document is presented to, or in the possession of, the attending physician at the time the decision to terminate a life-support system is made.

Nutrition and hydration. If the attending physician does not deem the patient to be in a terminal condition, beneficial medical treatment and nutrition and hydration must be provided.

Presumption of intent. This act creates no presumption concerning the wishes of a patient who has not executed a living will document as described in this act.

Comfort care. Notwithstanding the provisions of this act, comfort care and pain alleviation shall be provided in all cases.

Pregnancy. The provisions of this act shall not apply to a pregnant patient.

Qualifications. Any competent adult may execute a declaration authorizing the removal of a life-support system, to be signed by the declarant and witnessed and signed by 2 other individuals.

Form of declaration. The law specifies that the declaration shall be in "substantially" the same form as that listed in the Appendix. The addition of personalized instructions is not expressly forbidden by law.

DELAWARE: DEATH WITH DIGNITY ACT (1982)

Right of self-determination. An individual, legally adult (18 years of age or older), who is competent and of sound mind, has the right to refuse medical or surgical treatment if such refusal is not contrary to existing public health laws. Such individual has the right to make a written, dated declaration instructing any physician, including without limitation the treating physician, to cease or refrain from medical or surgical treatment should the declarant be in a terminal condition, as confirmed in writing by 2 physicians.

Appointment of agent. An adult person by written declaration may appoint an agent who will act on behalf of such appointor, if, due to a condition resulting from illness or injury and, in the judgment of the attending physician, the appointor becomes incapable of making a decision in the exercise of the right to accept or refuse medical treatment. An agent appointed in accordance with this section may accept or refuse medical treatment proposed by the appointor if, in the judgment of the attending physician, the appointor is incapable of making that decision. This authority shall include the right to refuse medical treatment which would extend the appointor's life. An agent authorized to make decisions under this act has a duty to act in good faith, and with due regard for the benefit and interests of the appointor.

Execution of declaration. Any adult person may execute a declaration directing the withholding or withdrawal of maintenance medical treatment, where the person is in a terminal condition and under such circumstances as may be set forth in the declaration. The declaration made pursuant to this act shall be: (1) In writing; (2) Signed by the person making the declaration or by another person in the declarant's presence and at the declarant's expressed direction; (3) Dated; and (4) Signed in the presence of 2 or more adult witnesses, meeting the qualifications described below.

Witnesses. The declaration shall be signed by the declarant in the presence of 2 subscribing witnesses, neither of whom: (1) Is related to the declarant by blood or marriage; (2) Is entitled to any portion of the estate of the declarant under any will of the declarant or codicil thereto then existing nor, at the time of the declaration, is entitled by operation of law then existing; (3) Has, at the time of the execution of the declaration, a present or inchoate claim against any portion of the estate of the declarant; (4) Has a direct financial responsibility for the declarant's medical care; or (5) Is an employee of the hospital or other health care facility in which the declarant is a patient. Each witness to the declaration shall state in writing that he is not prohibited by any of the above criteria from being a witness under this act.

Form of declaration. No particular required or recommended form is given in the Delaware statutes. For a copy of a generic Living Will form which meets the legal requirements of this state, see Appendix B.

Pregnancy. The declaration of a patient diagnosed as pregnant by the attending physician shall be of no effect during the course of the patient's pregnancy.

Defective declaration. When a declaration is lacking any requirement specified by this act and such defect is later corrected by amendment or codicil, whether formally or informally prepared, such declaration shall be valid ab initio (from the beginning), notwithstanding the earlier defect.

Revocation. The desires of a declarant who is competent shall at all times supersede the effect of the declaration. A declarant may revoke his declaration at any time, without regard to his mental state or competency. Any of the following methods is sufficient for revocation: (1) Destruction, cancellation, obliteration, or mutilation of the declaration with an intent to revoke it. If physical disability has rendered the declarant unable to destroy, cancel, obliterate, or mutilate the declaration, he may direct another individual to do so in his presence; (2) An oral statement made in the presence of 2 persons, each 18 years of age or older, which expresses an intent contrary to that expressed in the declaration; (3) Either a new declaration, made in the same manner with the same formality as the former declaration, which expresses an intent contrary to that expressed in the prior declaration; or a written revocation signed and dated by the declarant. There shall be no criminal nor civil liability on the part of any person for failure to act in accordance with a revocation, unless such person has actual or constructive knowledge of the revocation.

Presumption of validity. If the declarant is incompetent at the time of the decision to withhold or withdraw life-sustaining procedures, a declaration executed in accordance with this act is presumed to be valid. For purposes of this act, a physician or a health care facility may presume, in the absence of actual notice to the contrary, that an individual who executed a declaration was of sound mind when it was executed. The fact that an individual executed a declaration shall not be considered as an indication of such individual's mental incompetency.

Immunity. Physicians or nurses who act in reliance on a document executed in accordance with this act, where such health care personnel have no actual notice of revocation or contrary indication, by withholding medical procedures for an individual who executed such document shall be presumed to be acting in good faith, and unless negligent shall be immune from civil or criminal liability.

Safeguards. Anyone who has good reason to believe that the withdrawal or withholding of a maintenance medical treatment in a particular case: (1) Is contrary to the most recent expressed wishes of a declarant; (2) Is being proposed pursuant to a declaration that has been falsified, forged, or coerced; or (3) Is being considered without the benefit of a revocation which has been unlawfully concealed, destroyed, altered, or cancelled; may petition the Court of Chancery for appointment of a guardian for such declarant. The Division of Aging and the Public Guardian shall have oversight over any declaration executed by a resident of a sanatorium, rest home, nursing home, boarding home, or related institution as the same is defined in section 1101 of this title. Such declaration shall have no force nor effect if the declarant is a resident of a sanatorium, rest home, nursing home, boarding home, or related institution at the time the declaration is executed unless 1 of the witnesses is a person designated as a patient advocate or ombudsman by either the Division of Aging or the Public Guardian. The patient advocate or ombudsman must have the qualifications required of other witnesses under this act (see section on "Witnesses" above).

Declaration part of medical record. Upon receipt of a declaration, the hospital or the attending physician shall acknowledge receipt of same, and shall include the declaration as part of the declarant's medical records.

Suicide. Neither the execution of a declaration under this act nor the fact that maintenance medical treatment is withheld from a patient in accordance therewith shall, for any purpose, constitute a suicide.

Insurance. The making of a declaration pursuant to this act shall not restrict, inhibit, nor impair in any manner the sale, procurement, or issuance of any policy of life insurance, nor shall it be deemed or presumed to modify the terms of an existing policy of life insurance. No policy of life insurance shall be legally impaired or invalidated in any manner by the withholding or withdrawal of maintenance medical treatment from an insured patient, notwithstanding any term of the policy to the contrary.

Conditional execution of declaration. No physician, health facility, or other health care provider, nor any health care service plan, insurer issuing disability insurance, self-insured employee welfare benefit plan, or nonprofit hospital service plan shall require any person to execute a declaration as a condition of being insured, or for receiving health care services, nor shall the signing of a declaration be a bar.

Penalties. Whoever threatens directly or indirectly, coerces, or intimidates any person to execute a declaration directing the withholding or withdrawal of maintenance medical treatment shall be guilty of a misdemeanor and upon conviction shall be fined not less than $500 nor more than $1000; be imprisoned not less than 30 days nor more than 90 days; or both. The Superior Court shall have jurisdiction over such offenses. Whoever knowingly conceals, destroys, falsifies, or forges a document with intent to create the false impression that another person has directed that maintenance medical treatment be utilized for the prolongation of his life is guilty of a Class C felony. The Superior Court shall have jurisdiction over all offenses under this act.

Definition of maintenance medical treatment and comfort care. The term "maintenance medical treatment" as used in this act shall mean any medical or surgical procedure or intervention which utilizes mechanical or artificial means to sustain, restore, or supplant a vital function; and which would only serve to artificially prolong the dying process. The words "maintenance medical treatment" shall not include the administration of medication, nor the performance of any medical procedure necessary to provide comfort care or alleviate pain.

DISTRICT OF COLUMBIA: NATURAL DEATH ACT (1982)

Execution of declaration. Any person 18 years of age or older may execute a declaration directing the withholding or withdrawal of life-sustaining procedures from themselves should they be in a terminal condition. The declaration made pursuant to this act shall be : (1) In writing; (2) Signed by the person making the declaration or by another person in the declarant's presence at the declarant's express direction; (3) Dated; and (4) Signed in the presence of 2 or more witnesses at least 18 years of age.

Witnesses. A witness shall not be: (a) The person who signed the declaration on behalf of and at the direction of the declarant; (b) Related to the declarant by blood or marriage; (c) Entitled to any portion of the estate of the declarant according to the laws of intestate succession of the District of Columbia or under any will of the declarant or codicil thereto; (d) Directly financially responsible for declarant's medical care; or (e) The attending physician, an employee of the attending physician, or an employee of the health facility in which the declarant is a patient.

Notification of physician. It shall be the responsibility of the declarant to provide for notification to his or her attending physician of the existence of the declaration. An attending physician, when presented with the declaration, shall make the declaration or a copy of the declaration a part of the declarant's medical records.

Form of declaration. See Appendix. The declaration shall be substantially in this form, but in addition may include other specific directions not inconsistent with other provisions of this act.

Additional directions severable. Should any of the other specific directions added to the declaration be held to be invalid, such invalidity shall not affect other directions of the declaration which can be given effect without the invalid direction, and to this end the directions in the declaration are severable.

Definition of life-sustaining procedure; excluded treatments. The term "life-sustaining procedure" shall not include the administration of medication or the performance of any medical procedure deemed necessary to provide comfort care or to alleviate pain.

Restrictions. A declaration shall have no effect if the declarant is a patient in an intermediate care or skilled care facility as defined in the Health Care Facilities Regulation, enacted June 14, 1974 (Reg. 74-15; 20 DCR 1423) at the time the declaration is executed unless 1 of the 2 witnesses to the directive is a patient advocate or ombudsman. The patient advocate or ombudsman shall have the same qualifications as a witness under the section on "Witnesses" above.

Revocation. A declaration may be revoked at any time only by the declarant or at the express direction of the declarant without regard to the declarant's mental state by any of the following methods: (1) By being obliterated, burnt, torn, or otherwise destroyed or defaced by the declarant or by some person in the declarant's presence and at his or her direction; (2) By a written revocation of the declaration signed and dated by the declarant or person acting at the direction of the declarant. Such revocation shall become effective only upon communication of the revocation to the attending physician by the declarant or by a person acting on behalf of the declarant. The attending physician shall record in the patient's medical record the time and date when he or she receives notification of the written revocation; or (3) By a verbal expression of the intent to revoke the declaration, in the presence of a witness 18 years or older who signs and dates a writing confirming that such expression of intent was made. Any verbal revocation shall become effective only upon communication of the revocation to the attending physician by the declarant or by a person acting on behalf of the declarant. The attending physician shall record, in the patient's medical record, the time, date, and place of when he or she receives notification of the revocation. There shall be no criminal or civil liability on the part of any person for failure to act upon a revocation made pursuant to this section unless that person has actual knowledge of the revocation.

Physician's duty to confirm terminal condition. An attending physician who has been notified of the existence of a declaration executed under this act, without delay after the diagnosis of a terminal condition of the declarant, shall take the necessary steps to provide for written certification and confirmation of the declarant's terminal condition by 2 physicians who have personally examined the patient, one of whom shall be the attending physician, so that the declarant may be deemed to be a qualified patient under this act. Once written certification and confirmation of the declarant's terminal condition is made, a person becomes a qualified patient under this act only if the attending physician verbally or in writing informs the patient of his or her terminal condition and documents such communication in the patient's medical record. If the patient is diagnosed as unable to comprehend verbal or written communications, such patient shall become a qualified patient immediately upon written certification and confirmation of his or her terminal condition by the attending physician. An attending physician who does not comply with this section shall be considered to have committed an act of unprofessional conduct under section 2-1326.

Desires of patient supersede declaration. The desires of a qualified patient shall at all times supersede the effect of the declaration.

Presumption of validity. If the qualified patient is incompetent at the time of the decision to withhold or withdraw life-sustaining procedures, a declaration executed in accordance with this act is presumed to be valid. For the purpose of this act, a physician or health facility may presume in the absence of actual notice to the contrary that an individual who executed a declaration was of sound mind when it was executed. The fact of an individual's having executed a declaration shall not be considered as an indication of a declarant's mental incompetency.

Immunity. No physician, licensed health care professional, health facility, or employee thereof who in good faith and pursuant to reasonable medical standards causes or participates in the withholding or withdrawing of life-sustaining procedures from a qualified patient pursuant to a declaration made in accordance with this act shall, as a result thereof, be subject to criminal or civil liability, or be found to have committed an act of unprofessional conduct.

Transfer. An attending physician who cannot comply with the declaration of a qualified patient pursuant to this act shall, in conjunction with the next of kin of the patient or other responsible individual, effect the transfer of the qualified patient to another physician who will honor the declaration of the qualified patient. Transfer under these circumstances shall not constitute abandonment. Failure of an attending physician to effect the transfer of the qualified patient according to this section, in the event he or she cannot comply with the directive, shall constitute unprofessional conduct as defined in section 2-1326.

Penalties. Any person who willfully conceals, cancels, defaces, obliterates, or damages the declaration of another without the declarant's consent or who falsifies or forges a revocation of the declaration of another shall commit an offense, and upon conviction shall be fined an amount not to exceed $5,000 or be imprisoned for a period not to exceed 3 years, or both. Any person who falsifies or forges the declaration of another, or willfully conceals or withholds personal knowledge of the revocation of a declaration, with the intent to cause a withholding or withdrawal of life-sustaining procedures, contrary to the wishes of the declarant, and thereby, because of such act, directly causes life-sustaining procedures to be withheld or withdrawn and death to be hastened, shall be subject to prosecution for unlawful homicide pursuant to section 22-2401.

Suicide. The withholding or withdrawal of life-sustaining procedures from a qualified patient in accordance with the provisions of this act shall not, for any purpose, constitute a suicide and shall not constitute the crime of assisting suicide.

   Insurance.   The making of a declaration pursuant to this act shall not
affect in any manner the sale, procurement, or issuance of any policy of life
insurance, nor   shall it be deemed to modify the terms of an existing policy of
life insurance. No policy of life insurance shall be legally impaired or
invalidated in any manner by the withholding or withdrawal of life-sustaining
procedures from an insured qualified patient, notwithstanding any term of the
policy to the contrary.

   Conditional execution of declaration.   No physician, health facility, or
other health care provider, and no health care service plan, health maintenance organization, insurer issuing disability insurance, self-insured employee
welfare benefit plan, nonprofit medical service corporation, or mutual nonprofit hospital service corporation shall require any person to execute a
declaration as a condition for being insured for, or receiving, health care
services.

   Preservation of existing rights.   Nothing in this act shall impair or
supersede any legal right or legal responsibility which any person may have to
effect the withholding or withdrawal of life-sustaining procedures in any
lawful manner. In such respect the provisions of this act are cumulative.

   Presumption of intent.   This act shall create no presumption concerning
the intention of an individual who has not executed a declaration to consent to
the use or withholding of life-sustaining procedures in the event of a terminal
condition.

   Mercy killing.   Nothing in this act shall be construed to condone,
authorize, or approve mercy killing or to permit any affirmative or deliberate
act or omission to end a human life other than to permit the natural process of
dying as provided in this act.

FLORIDA: LIFE-PROLONGING PROCEDURE ACT (1984)

   Policy statement. The legislature finds that every competent adult has
the fundamental right to control the decisions relating to his own medical
care, including the decision to have provided, withheld, or withdrawn the
medical or surgical means or procedures calculated to prolong his life. This
right is subject to certain interests of society, such as the protection of
human life and the preservation of ethical standards in the medical profession. The legislature further finds that the artificial prolongation of
life for a person with a terminal condition may secure for him only a precarious and burdensome existence, while providing nothing medically necessary or
beneficial to the patient. In order that the rights and intentions of a person
with such. a condition may be respected even after he is no longer able to
participate actively in decisions concerning himself, and to encourage communication among such patient, his family, and his physician, the legislature
declares that the laws of this state recognize the right of a competent adult
to make an oral or written declaration instructing his physician to provide,
withhold, or withdraw life-prolonging procedures, or to designate another to
make the treatment decision for him, in the event that such person should be
diagnosed as suffering from a terminal condition.

   Execution of declaration.   Any competent adult may, at any time, make a written declaration directing the withholding or withdrawal of life-prolonging procedures in the event such person should have a terminal condition. A written declaration must be signed by the declarant in the presence of 2 subscribing witnesses, one of whom is neither a spouse nor a blood relative of the declarant. If the declarant is physically unable to sign the written declaration, his declaration may be given orally, in which event one of the witnesses must subscribe the declarant's signature in the declarant's presence and at the declarant's direction.

Notification of physician. It is the responsibility of the declarant to provide notification to his attending physician that the declaration has been made. In the event the declarant is comatose, incompetent, or otherwise mentally or physically incapable, any other person may notify the physician of the existence of the declaration. An attending physician who is so notified shall promptly make the declaration or a copy of the declaration, if the declaration is written, a part of the declarant's medical records. If the declaration is oral, the physician shall likewise promptly make the fact of such declaration a part of the patient's medical record.

Suggested form of declaration. See Appendix. The declaration may, but need not be, in this form.

Definition of life-sustaining procedure; excluded treatments. The term "life-sustaining procedure" does not include the provision of sustenance or the administration of medication or performance of any medical procedure deemed necessary to provide comfort care or to alleviate pain.

Addition of specific directions permitted. A declaration executed according to this act may include other specific directions, including, but not limited to, a designation of another person to make the treatment decision for the declarant should he be diagnosed as suffering from a terminal condition and comatose, incompetent, or otherwise mentally or physically incapable of communication. Should any other specific direction be held to be invalid, such invalidity will not affect the declaration.

Revocation. A declaration may be revoked at any time by the declarant: (1) By means of a signed, dated writing; (2) By means of the physical cancellation or destruction of the declaration by the declarant or by another in the declarant's presence and at the declarant's direction; or (3) By means of an oral expression of intent to revoke. Any such revocation will be effective when it is communicated to the attending physician. No civil or criminal liability shall be imposed upon any person for a failure to act upon a revocation unless that person has actual knowledge of such revocation.

Procedure in absence of declaration. Life-prolonging procedures may be withheld or withdrawn from an adult patient with a terminal condition who is comatose, incompetent, or otherwise physically or mentally incapable of communication and has not made a declaration in accordance with this act, if there are a consultation and a written agreement for the withholding or withdrawal of life-prolonging procedures between the attending physician and any of the following individuals, who shall be guided by the express or implied intentions of the patient, in the following order of priority if no individual in a prior class is reasonably available, willing, and competent to act: (a) The judicially appointed guardian of the person of the patient if such guardian has been appointed. This paragraph shall not be construed to require such appointment before a treatment decision can be made under this section. (b) The person or persons designated by the patient in writing to make the treatment decision for him should he be diagnosed as suffering from a terminal condition. (c) The patient's spouse. (d) An adult child of the patient or, if the patient has more than one adult child, a majority of the adult children who are reasonably available for consultation. (e) The parents of the patient. (f) The nearest living relative of the patient. In any case in which the treatment decision is made, at least 2 witnesses must be present at the time of the consultation when the treatment decision is made.

Presumption of intent. The absence of a declaration by an adult patient does not give rise to any presumption as to his intent to consent to, or refuse, life-prolonging procedures.

Pregnancy. The declaration of a qualified patient, or the written agreement for a patient qualified according to the "Procedures in Absence of Declaration" outlined above, which patient has been diagnosed as pregnant by the attending physician, shall have no effect during the course of the pregnancy.

Transfer. An attending physician who refuses to comply with the declaration of a qualified patient who has been diagnosed and certified in writing by the attending physician and by one other physician who has examined the patient to be afflicted with a terminal condition, or the treatment decision of a person designated to make the decision by the declarant in his declaration pursuant to the "Procedure in Absence of Declaration" outlined above, shall make a reasonable effort to transfer the patient to another physician.

Immunity from liability. A health care facility, physician, or other person who acts under the direction of a physician is not subject to criminal prosecution or civil liability, and will not be deemed to have engaged in unprofessional conduct, as a result of the withholding or withdrawal of life-prolonging procedures from a patient with a terminal condition in accordance with this act. A person who authorizes the withholding or withdrawal of life-prolonging procedures from a patient with a terminal condition in accordance with a qualified patient's declaration or as provided in the "Procedure in Absence of Declaration" is not subject to criminal prosecution or civil liability for such action. The provisions of this section shall apply unless it is shown by a preponderance of the evidence that the person authorizing or effectuating the withholding or withdrawal of life-prolonging procedures did not, in good faith, comply with the provisions of this act. A declaration made in accordance with this act shall be presumed to have been made voluntarily.

Mercy killing. Nothing in this act shall be construed to condone, authorize, or approve mercy killing or euthanasia, or to permit any affirmative or deliberate act or omission to end life other than to permit the natural process of dying.

Suicide. The withholding or withdrawal of life-prolonging procedures from a patient in accordance with the provisions of this act does not, for any purpose, constitute a suicide.

Insurance. The making of a declaration pursuant to this act shall not affect the sale, procurement, or issuance or any policy of life insurance, nor shall such making of a declaration be deemed to modify the terms of an existing policy of life insurance. No policy of life insurance will be legally impaired or invalidated by the withholding or withdrawal of life-prolonging procedures from an insured patient in accordance with the provisions of this act, notwithstanding any term of the policy to the contrary.

Conditional execution of declaration. A person shall not be required to make a declaration as a condition for being insured for, or receiving, health care services.

Penalties. Any person who willfully conceals, cancels, defaces, obliterates, or damages the declaration of another without the declarant's consent or who falsifies or forges a revocation of the declaration of another, and who thereby causes life-prolonging procedures to be utilized in contravention of the previously expressed intent of the patient, is guilty of a felony of the third degree, punishable as provided in section 775.082, section 775.083, or section 775.084. Any person who falsifies or forges the declaration of another or who willfully conceals or withholds personal knowledge of the revocation of a declaration, with the intent to cause a withholding or withdrawal of life-prolonging procedures contrary to the wishes of the declarant, and who thereby because of such act directly causes life-prolonging procedures to be withheld or withdrawn and death to be hastened, is guilty of a felony of the second degree, punishable as provided in section 775.082, section 775.083, or section 775.084.

Existing declaration. The declaration of any patient made prior to the effective date of this act (October 1, 1984) shall be given effect as provided in this act.

Preservation of existing rights. The provisions of this act are cumulative to the existing law regarding an individual's right to consent, or refuse to consent, to medical treatment and do not impair any existing rights or responsibilities which a health care provider, a patient, including a minor or incompetent patient, or a patient's family may have in regard to the withholding or withdrawal of life-prolonging medical procedures under the common law or statutes of the state.

GEORGIA: LIVING WILL ACT (1984; amended 1985)

Policy statement. The General Assembly finds that modern medical technology has made possible the artificial prolongation of human life. The General Assembly further finds that, in the interest of protecting individual autonomy, such prolongation of life for persons with a terminal condition may cause loss of patient dignity and unnecessary pain and suffering, while providing nothing medically necessary or beneficial to the patient. The General Assembly further finds that there exists considerable uncertainty in the medical and legal professions as to the legality of terminating the use of life-sustaining procedures in certain situations. In recognition of the dignity and privacy which patients have a right to expect, the General Assembly declares that the laws of the State of Georgia shall recognize the right of a competent adult person to make a written directive, known as a living will, instructing his physician to withhold or withdraw life-sustaining procedures in the event of a terminal condition.

Execution of declaration. Any competent adult at least 18 years of age may execute a document directing that, should the declarant have a terminal condition, as diagnosed and certified in writing by 2 physicians after personally examining the declarant, life-sustaining procedures be withheld or withdrawn.

Witnesses. Such living will shall be signed by the declarant in the presence of at least 2 competent adult witnesses who, at the time of the execution of the living will, to their best of their knowledge: (1) Are not related to the declarant by blood or marriage; (2) Would not be entitled to any portion of the estate of the declarant upon the declarant's decease under any testamentary will of the declarant, or codicil thereto, and would not be entitled to any such portion by operation of law under the rules of descent and distribution of this state at the time of the execution of the living will; (3) Are neither the attending physician nor an employee of the attending physician nor an employee of the hospital or skilled nursing facility in which the declarant is a patient; (4) Are not directly financially responsible for the declarant's medical care; and (5) Do not have a claim against any portion of the estate of the declarant.

Required form of declaration. The declaration shall be a document, separate and self-contained, and in the exact form as that given in the Appendix.

Definition of life-sustaining procedures; excluded treatments. The term "life-sustaining procedure" shall not include nourishment or the administration of medication to alleviate pain or the performance of any medical procedure deemed necessary to alleviate pain.

Allowance for personalized instructions in declaration. None.

Patients in hospitals or skilled nursing facilities. A living will shall have no force or effect if the declarant is a patient in a hospital or skilled nursing facility at the time the living will is executed unless the living will is signed in the presence of the 2 witnesses as provided in the section on "Witnesses" above and, additionally, is signed in the presence of either the chief of the hospital medical staff, if witnessed in a hospital, or the medical director, if witnessed in a skilled nursing facility.

Revocation. A living will may be revoked at any time by the declarant, without regard to his mental state or competency, by any of the following methods: (1) By being canceled, defaced, obliterated, burnt, torn, or otherwise destroyed by the declarant or by some person in his presence and by his direction; (2) By the declarant or a person acting at the direction of the declarant signing and dating a written revocation expressing the intent of the declarant to revoke. Such revocation shall become effective only upon communication to the attending physician by the declarant or by a person acting at the direction of the declarant. The attending physician shall record in the patient's medical record the time and date when he received notification of the written revocation; or (3) By any verbal or nonverbal expression by the declarant of his intent to revoke the living will. Such revocation shall become effective only upon communication to the attending physician by the declarant or by a person acting at the direction of the declarant. The attending physician shall record in the patient's medical record the time, date, and place of the revocation and the time, date, and place, if different, when he received notification of the revocation. Any person who participates in the withholding or withdrawal of life-sustaining procedures pursuant to a living will, as authorized by this act, which person has actual knowledge that such living will has been properly revoked, shall not have any civil or criminal immunity otherwise granted under this act for such conduct.

Period of effectiveness. A living will shall be effective for a period of 7 years from the date of execution thereof unless sooner revoked in a manner prescribed in the section on "Revocation" above. If the declarant of an unrevoked living will becomes incapable of communicating with the attending physician, the living will shall remain in effect beyond such 7-year period until such time as the declarant is able to communicate with the attending physician. Nothing in this act shall be construed to prevent a declarant from reexecuting a living will at any time in accordance with the formalities of this act. If the declarant has executed more than one living will, such 7-year period shall be determined from the date of execution of the last living will known to the attending physician.

Immunity of participants from liability. No physician nor any person acting under his direction and no hospital, skilled nursing facility, nor any agent or employee thereof who, acting in good faith in accordance with the requirements of this act, causes the withholding or withdrawal of life-sustaining procedures from a patient or who otherwise participates in good faith therein shall be subject to any civil liability therefor. No physician nor any person acting under his direction and no hospital, skilled nursing facility, nor any agent or employee thereof who, acting in good faith in accordance with the requirements of this act, causes the withholding or withdrawal of life-sustaining procedures from a patient or who otherwise participates in good faith therein shall be guilty of any criminal act therefor, nor shall any such person be guilty of unprofessional conduct therefor. No person who witnesses and attests a living will in good faith and in accordance with this act shall be civilly or criminally liable or guilty of unprofessional conduct for such action.

Conditions precedent to withholding or withdrawal of life-sustaining procedures. Prior to effecting a withholding or withdrawal of life-sustaining procedures from a patient pursuant to a living will, the attending physician: (1) Shall determine that, to the best of his knowledge, the declarant patient is not pregnant; (2) Shall, without delay after the diagnosis of a terminal condition of the declarant, take the necessary steps to provide for written certification by said physician of the declarant's terminal condition; (3) Shall make a reasonable effort to determine that the living will complies with the form prescribed by this act; and (4) Shall make the living will and the written certification of the terminal condition a part of the declarant patient's medical records.

Presumption of validity. The living will shall be presumed, unless revoked, to be the directions of the declarant regarding the withholding or withdrawal of life-sustaining procedures.

Transfer procedure. No person shall be civilly liable for failing or refusing in good faith to effectuate the living will of the declarant patient. The attending physician who fails or refuses to comply with the declaration of a patient pursuant to this act shall endeavor to advise promptly the next of kin or legal guardian of the declarant that such physician is unwilling to effectuate the living will of the declarant patient. The attending physician shall thereafter at the election of the next of kin or the legal guardian of the declarant: (1) Make a good faith attempt to effect the transfer of the qualified patient to another physician who will effectuate the declaration of the patient; or (2) Permit the next of kin or legal guardian to obtain another physician who will effectuate the declaration of the patient.

Suicide. The making of a living will pursuant to this act shall not, for any purpose, constitute a suicide.

Insurance. The making of a living will pursuant to this act shall not restrict, inhibit, or impair in any manner the sale, procurement, issuance, or enforceability of any policy of life insurance, nor shall it be deemed to modify the terms of an existing policy of life insurance. No policy of life insurance shall be legally impaired or invalidated in any manner by the making of a living will pursuant to this act or by the withholding or withdrawal of life-sustaining procedures from an insured patient, nor shall the making of such a living will or the withholding or withdrawal of such life-sustaining procedures operate to deny any additional insurance benefits for accidental death of the patient in any case in which the terminal condition of the patient is the result of accident, notwithstanding any term of the policy to the contrary.

<u>Conditional execution of declaration.</u> No physician, hospital, skilled nursing facility, or other health provider, and no health care service plan, insurer issuing disability insurance, self-insured employee welfare benefit plan, or nonprofit hospital service plan shall require any person to execute a living will as a condition for being insured for, or receiving, health care services.

<u>Restriction on health care facilities' preparing living wills.</u> No hospital, skilled nursing facility, or other medical or health care facility shall prepare, offer to prepare, or otherwise provide forms for living wills unless specifically requested to do so by a person desiring to execute a living will.

<u>Penalties.</u> Any person who willfully conceals, cancels, defaces, obliterates, alters, or damages the living will of another without such declarant's consent or who witnesses a living will knowing at the time he is not eligible to witness such living will under the provisions of this act or who coerces or attempts to coerce a person into making a living will shall be guilty of a misdemeanor. Any person who falsifies or forges the living will of another or willfully conceals or withholds personal knowledge of a revocation as provided in this act with the intent to cause a withholding or withdrawal of life-sustaining procedures contrary to the wishes of the declarant and, thereby, because of any such action, directly causes life-sustaining procedures to be withheld or withdrawn and death thereby to be hastened shall be subject to prosecution for criminal homicide as provided in Chapter 5 of Title 16.

<u>Effect of this act on other legal rights and duties.</u> Nothing in this act shall impair or supersede any legal right or legal responsibility which any person may have to effect the withholding or withdrawal of life-sustaining procedures in any lawful manner. In such respect the provisions of this act are cumulative.

<u>Mercy killing.</u> Nothing in this act shall be construed to condone, authorize, or approve mercy killing or to permit any affirmative or deliberate act or omission to end life other than to permit the process of dying as provided in this act. Furthermore, nothing in this act shall be construed to condone, authorize, or approve abortion.

<u>Presumption of intent.</u> This act shall create no presumption concerning the intention of an individual who has not executed a declaration to consent to the use or withholding of life-sustaining procedures in the event of a terminal condition.

<u>Construction of this act in relation to Title 53.</u> This act is wholly independent of the provisions of Title 53, relating to wills, trusts, and the administration of estates, and nothing in this act shall be construed to affect in any way the provisions of said Title 53.

IDAHO: NATURAL DEATH ACT (1977)

Statement policy. The legislature finds that adult persons have the fundamental right to control the decisions relating to the rendering of their medical care, including the decision to have life-sustaining procedures withheld or withdrawn in instances of a terminal condition. The legislature further finds that modern medical technology has made possible the artificial prolongation of human life beyond natural limits. The legislature further finds that patients suffering from terminal conditions are sometimes unable to express their desire to withhold or withdraw such artificial life-prolongation procedures which provide nothing medically necessary or beneficial to the patient because of the progress of the disease process which renders the patient comatose or unable to communicate with the physician. In recognition of the dignity and privacy which patients have a right to expect, the legislature hereby declares that the laws of this state shall recognize the right of an adult person to make a written directive instructing his physician to withhold or withdraw life-sustaining procedures when such person is suffering from a terminal condition and unable to instruct his physician regarding such procedures because of the terminal condition.

Execution of directive for withholding life-sustaining procedures. Any qualified patient of sound mind and at least 18 years old who has been diagnosed by the attending physician to be afflicted with a terminal condition may execute a directive directing the withholding or withdrawal of artificial life-sustaining procedures when such patient becomes unconscious or unable to communicate with his attending physician because of the progress of the terminal condition resulting in his inability to voluntarily determine whether such procedures should be utilized, and if such procedures would serve only to prolong the moment of his death, and where his attending physician determines that his death is imminent whether or not such procedures are utilized.

Witnesses. The directive shall be signed by the qualified patient in the presence of 2 witnesses who shall verify in such directive that they are not related to the qualified patient by blood or marriage, that they would not be entitled to any portion of the estate of the qualified patient upon his demise under any will of the qualified patient or codicil thereto then existing, at the time of the directive, or by operation of law then existing (as an heir by intestate succession). In addition, the witnesses shall verify that they are not the attending physician, an employee of the attending physician or a health facility in which the qualified patient is a patient, or any person who has a claim against any portion of the estate of the qualified patient upon his demise at the time of the execution of the directive.

Required form of directive. See Appendix for the precise wording of the form as specified by the Idaho statutes.

Revocation. A directive may be revoked at any time by the qualified patient, without regard to his mental state of competence, by any of the following methods: (a) By being cancelled, defaced, obliterated or burned, torn, or otherwise destroyed by the qualified patient or by some person in his presence and by his direction. (b) By a written revocation of the qualified patient expressing his intent to revoke, signed by the qualified patient. (c) By a verbal expression by the qualified patient of his intent to revoke the directive. There shall be no criminal or civil liability on the part of any person for failure to act upon a revocation of a directive made pursuant to this section unless that person has actual knowledge of the revocation.

Expiration of directive. A directive shall be effective for 5 years from the date of execution unless sooner revoked in a manner described in the section on "Revocation" above. Nothing in this act shall be construed to prevent a qualified patient from reexecuting a directive at any time. If the qualified patient becomes comatose or is rendered incapable of communicating with the attending physician, the directive shall remain in effect for the duration of the comatose condition or until such time as the qualified patient's condition renders him able to communicate with the attending physician.

Immunity. No physician or health facility, which, acting in accordance with a directive meeting the requirements of this act, causes the withholding or withdrawal of artificial life-sustaining procedures from a qualified patient, shall be subject to civil liability or criminal liability therefrom.

General provisions. This act shall have no effect or be in any manner construed to apply to persons not executing a directive pursuant to this act nor shall it in any manner affect the rights of any such persons or of others acting for or on behalf of such persons to give or refuse to give consent or withhold consent for any medical care; neither shall this act be construed to affect chapter 43, title 39, Idaho Code, in any manner.

Insurance. The making of a directive pursuant to this act shall not restrict, inhibit, or impair in any manner the sale, procurement, or issuance of any policy of life insurance, nor shall it be deemed to modify the terms of an existing policy of life insurance. No policy of life insurance shall be legally impaired or invalidated in any manner by the withholding or withdrawal of artificial life-sustaining procedures from an insured qualified patient, notwithstanding any term of the policy to the contrary.

Conditional execution of directive. No physician, health facility, or other health provider and no health care service plan, insurer issuing disability insurance, self-insured employee welfare benefit plan, or nonprofit hospital service plan, shall require any person to execute a directive as a condition for being insured for, or receiving, health care services.

Definition of life-sustaining procedures and alleviation of pain. The term "artificial life-sustaining procedures" as used in this act shall not include the administration of medication or the performance of any medical procedure deemed necessary to alleviate pain.

Provisions of act severable. The provisions of this act are declared to be severable and if any provision of this act or the application of such provision to any person or circumstance is declared invalid for any reason, such declaration shall not affect the validity of remaining portions of this act.

ILLINOIS: LIVING WILL ACT (1984)

Policy statement. The legislature finds that persons have the fundamental right to control the decisions relating to the rendering of their own medical care, including the decision to have life-sustaining procedures withheld or withdrawn in instances of a terminal condition. In order that the rights of patients may be respected even after they are no longer able to participate actively in decisions about themselves, the legislature hereby declares that the laws of this state shall recognize the right of a person to make a written

declaration instructing his or her physician to withhold or withdraw life-sustaining procedures in the event of a terminal condition.

Execution of a declaration. An individual of sound mind and having
reached the age of majority (18) or having obtained the status of an emanci-
pated person pursuant to the "Emancipation of Mature Minors Act," as now or
hereafter amended, may execute a declaration directing that if he is suffering
from a terminal condition, then life-sustaining procedures shall not be
utilized for the prolongation of his life.

Validity of declaration. A declaration is not valid unless it has been
executed with the same formalities as required of a valid will pursuant to the
Probate Act of 1975, that is, it must be in writing, signed and dated by the
declarant, and witnessed by 2 individuals. The declaration may also be signed
by another person at the direction of the declarant, in the event the declarant
is unable to sign the document himself.

Witnesses. Neither of the witnesses to a declaration may be the same
person who signed the declaration for or at the direction of the declarant.
Neither may be related to the declarant by blood or marriage, entitled to any
portion of the estate of the declarant according to the laws of intestate
succession or under any will of the declarant or codicil thereto, or directly
financially responsible for the declarant's medical care.

Recommended form of declaration. See Appendix. Although the declaration
shall be substantially in the form given, in addition it may include other
specific directions.

Additional directions severable. Should any of the other specific
directions which are added be held to be invalid, such invalidity shall not
affect other directions of the declaration which can be given effect without
the invalid direction; to this end, the directions in the declaration are
severable.

Definition of life-sustaining procedure; exclusions. "Life-sustaining
procedure" shall not include the administration of medication or sustenance or
the performance of any medical procedure deemed necessary to provide comfort
care or to alleviate pain.

Pregnancy. The declaration of a qualified patient diagnosed as pregnant
by the attending physician shall have no effect during the course of the
patient's pregnancy.

Notification of physician. It shall be the responsibility of the patient
to provide for notification to his or her attending physician of the existence
of the declaration. An attending physician who is so notified shall make the
declaration, or copy of the declaration, a part of the patient's medical
records.

Definition of qualified patient; verification of terminal illness.
"Qualified patient" means a patient who has executed a declaration in accordance with this act and who has been diagnosed and verified in writing to be
afflicted with a terminal condition by his or her attending physician who has
personally examined the patient. A physician who verifies in writing a
terminal condition under this act is presumed to be acting in good faith.
Unless it is alleged and proved that his action violated the standard of
reasonable professional care and judgment under the circumstances, he is immune
from civil or criminal liability that otherwise might be incurred.

Revocation. A declaration may be revoked at any time by the declarant by
any of the following methods: (1) By being obliterated, burnt, torn, or
otherwise destroyed or defaced in a manner indicating intention to cancel; (2)

By a written revocation of the declaration signed and dated by the declarant or person acting at the direction of the declarant; (3) By an oral expression of the intent to revoke the declaration, in the presence of a witness 18 years of age or older who signs and dates a writing confirming that such expression of intent was made. Any oral revocation shall become effective upon receipt by the attending physician of the above mentioned writing. The attending physician shall record in the patient's medical record the time, date, and place of when he or she received notification of the revocation.

Physician's responsibility. An attending physician who has been notified of the existence of a declaration executed under this act, without delay after the diagnosis of a terminal condition of the patient, shall take the necessary steps to provide for written verification of the patient's terminal condition, so that the patient may be deemed to be a qualified patient under this act.

Transfer. If a physician, because of his or her personal beliefs or conscience, is unable to comply with the terms of the declaration, the qualified patient or the family of the qualified patient, may request the case be referred to another physician. An attending physician who, because of his or her personal beliefs or conscience, is unable to comply with the declaration pursuant to this act shall, without delay, make the necessary arrangements to effect the transfer of the qualified patient, and the appropriate medical records that qualify said patient to another physician who has been identified by the qualified patient or by the family of the qualified patient, for effectuation of the qualified patient's declaration.

Primacy of patient's desire. The desires of a qualified patient shall at all times supersede the effect of the declaration.

Presumption of validity. If the qualified patient is incompetent at the time of the decision to withhold or withdraw life-sustaining procedures, a declaration executed in accordance with this act is presumed to be valid. For the purpose of this act, a physician or medical care facility may presume in the absence of actual notice to the contrary that an individual who executed a declaration was of sound mind when it was executed. The fact of an individual's having executed a declaration shall not be considered as an indication of a declarant's mental incompetency. Age of itself shall not be a bar to a determination of competency.

Immunity. No physician, licensed health care professional, medical care facility, or employee thereof who in good faith and pursuant to reasonable medical standards causes or participates in the withholding or withdrawing of life-sustaining procedures from a qualified patient pursuant to a declaration which purports to have been made in accordance with this act shall, as a result thereof, be subject to criminal or civil liability or be found to have committed an act of unprofessional conduct.

Penalties. Any person who willfully conceals, cancels, defaces, obliterates, or damages the declaration of another without such declarant's consent or who falsifies or forges a revocation of the declaration of another shall be civilly liable. Any person who falsifies or forges the declaration of another, or willfully conceals or withholds personal knowledge of a revocation, with the intent to cause a withholding or withdrawal of life-sustaining procedures contrary to the wishes of the qualified patient and thereby, because of such action, directly causes life-sustaining procedures to be withheld or withdrawn and death to another thereby be hastened, shall be subject to prosecution for involuntary manslaughter.

Suicide. The withholding or withdrawal of life-sustaining procedures from a qualified patient in accordance with the provisions of this act shall not, for any purpose, constitute a suicide.

Insurance. The making of a declaration pursuant to this act shall not affect in any manner the sale, procurement, or issuance of any policy of life insurance, nor shall it be deemed to modify the terms of an existing policy of life insurance. No policy of life insurance shall be legally impaired or invalidated in any manner by the withholding or withdrawal of life-sustaining procedures from an insured qualified patient, notwithstanding any term of the policy to the contrary.

Conditional execution of declaration. No physician, medical care facility, or other health care provider, and no health care service plan, health maintenance organization, insurer issuing disability insurance, self-insured employee welfare benefit plan, nonprofit medical service corporation, or mutual nonprofit hospital service corporation shall require any person to execute a declaration as a condition for being insured for, or receiving, health care services.

Cumulative effect of provisions. Nothing in this act shall impair or supersede any legal right or legal responsibility which any person may have to effect the withholding or withdrawal of life-sustaining procedures in any lawful manner. In such respect the provisions of this act are cumulative.

Presumption of intent. This act shall create no presumption concerning the intention of an individual who has not executed a declaration to consent to the use or withholding of life-sustaining procedures in the event of a terminal condition.

Mercy killing. Nothing in this act shall be construed to condone or approve mercy killing or to permit any affirmative or deliberate act or omission to end life other than to permit the natural process of dying as provided in this act.

INDIANA: LIVING WILLS AND LIFE-PROLONGING PROCEDURES ACT (1985)

Policy statement. Competent adults have the right to control the decisions relating to their own medical care, including the decision to have medical or surgical means or procedures calculated to prolong their lives provided, withheld, or withdrawn.

Consent to medical treatment. Any competent person may consent to or refuse consent for medical treatment, including life-prolonging procedures.

Immunity from liability. No health care provider is obligated to provide medical treatment to a patient who has refused medical treatment under the above section. No civil or criminal liability is imposed upon a health care provider for the failure to provide medical treatment to a patient who has refused the treatment in accordance with the above section.

Who may execute declaration. A person who is of sound mind and is at least 18 years of age may execute a life-prolonging procedures will declaration (to have life-sustaining procedures administered and continued) or a living will declaration (to have life-sustaining procedures withheld or withdrawn).

Requirements of declaration. Both types of declarations must be voluntary, in writing, signed by the person making the declaration or by another person in the declarant's presence and at the declarant's express direction, dated, and signed in the presence of at least 2 competent witnesses who are at least 18 years of age.

Witnesses. A witness to a living will declaration may not be (a) the person who signed the declaration on behalf of and at the direction of the declarant; (b) a parent, spouse, or child of the declarant; (c) entitled to any part of the declarant's estate whether the declarant dies with a will (testate) or without a will (intestate), including whether the witness could take from the declarant's estate if the declarant's will is declared invalid; or (d) directly financially responsible for the declarant's medical care. Note: For the purpose of subdivision (c), a person is not considered to be entitled to any part of the declarant's estate solely by virtue of being nominated as a personal representative or as the attorney for the estate in the declarant's will.

Pregnancy. The living will declaration of a person diagnosed as pregnant by the attending physician has no effect during the person's pregnancy.

Notification and recording of declaration. The life-prolonging procedures will declarant or the living will declarant shall notify the declarant's attending physician of the existence of the declaration. An attending physician who is so notified shall make the declaration or a copy of the declaration a part of the declarant's medical records.

Obligatory force of respective declarations. A living will declaration does not obligate the physician to use, withhold, or withdraw life-prolonging procedures but is presumptive evidence of the patient's desires concerning the use, withholding, or withdrawal of life-prolonging procedures under this act, and shall be given great weight by the physician in determining the intent of the patient now incompetent. A life-prolonging procedures will declaration does obligate the physician to use life-prolonging procedures as requested.

Recommended Form of Living Will Declaration and Life-Prolonging Procedures Declaration. See Appendix for the suggested form of each declaration. Although a declaration must be substantially in this form, it may include additional, specific directions. The invalidity of any additional, specific directions does not affect the validity of the declaration.

Definition of life-prolonging procedure; excluded treatments. "Life-prolonging procedure" does not include the provision of appropriate nutrition and hydration, the administration of medication, or the performance of any medical procedure necessary to provide comfort care or to alleviate pain.

Revocation. A living will declaration or a life-prolonging procedures will declaration may be revoked at any time by the declarant by (1) A signed, dated writing; (2) Physical cancellation or destruction of the declaration by the declarant or another in the declarant's presence and at the declarant's direction; or (3) An oral expression of the intent to revoke. A revocation is effective when communicated to the attending physician. No civil or criminal liability is imposed upon a person for failure to act upon a revocation unless the person had actual knowledge of the revocation. The revocation of a life-prolonging procedures will declaration is not evidence that the declarant desires to have life-prolonging procedures withheld or withdrawn.

Certification. The attending physician shall immediately certify in writing that a person is a qualified patient if the attending physician has diagnosed the patient as having a terminal condition, determined that the patient's death will occur from the terminal condition whether or not life-prolonging procedures are used, and the patient has executed a living will declaration or a life-prolonging procedures will declaration in accordance with this act and was of sound mind at the time of the execution. The attending physician shall include a copy of the certificate in the patient's medical records.

Immunity. It is lawful for the attending physician to withhold or withdraw life-prolonging procedures from a qualified patient if that patient properly executed a living will declaration under this act. A health care provider or an employee under the direction of a health care provider who in good faith and in accordance with reasonable medical standards participates in the withholding or withdrawal of life-prolonging procedures from a qualified patient who has executed a living will declaration in accordance with this act is not subject to criminal or civil liability and may not be found to have committed an act of unprofessional conduct.

Transfers. An attending physician who refuses to use, withhold, or withdraw life-prolonging procedures from a qualified patient shall transfer the patient to another physician who will honor the patient's living will declaration or life-prolonging procedures will declaration unless: (1) the physician has reason to believe the declaration was not validly executed or there is evidence that the patient no longer intends the declaration to be enforced; and (2) the patient is presently unable to validate the declaration. If the attending physician, after reasonable investigation, finds no other physician willing to honor the patient's declaration, the attending physician may refuse to withhold or withdraw life-prolonging procedures.

Validation of declaration. If the attending physician does not transfer a patient for the reason set forth in the section above, the physician shall attempt to ascertain the patient's intention and attempt to determine the validity of the declaration by consulting with any of the following individuals who are reasonably available, willing, and competent to act: (1) The judicially appointed guardian of the person of the patient if one has been appointed. This subdivision shall not be construed to require the appointment of a guardian in order that a treatment decision can be made under this section. (2) The person or persons designated by the patient in writing to make the treatment decision for the patient should the patient be diagnosed as suffering from a terminal condition. (3) The patient's spouse. (4) An adult child of the patient or, if the patient has more than 1 adult child, by a majority of the children who are reasonably available for consultation. (5) The parents of the patient. (6) An adult sibling of the patient or, if the patient has more than 1 adult sibling, by a majority of the siblings who are reasonably available for consultation. (7) The patient's clergy or others with firsthand knowledge of the patient's intention. The individuals described in subdivisions (1) through (7) shall act in the best interest of the patient and shall be guided by the patient's express or implied intentions, if known. The physician shall list the names in the patient's medical records of the individuals described in the subsections above who were consulted and the information received. If the attending physician determines from the information received under the subsections above that the qualified patient intended to execute a valid living will declaration, the physician may either withhold or withdraw life-prolonging procedures, with the concurrence of 1 other physician, as documented in the patient's medical records; or request a court of competent jurisdiction to appoint a guardian for the patient to make the consent decision on behalf of the patient.

Presumptions. If the qualified patient who executed a living will is incompetent at the time of the decision to withhold or withdraw life-prolonging procedures, a living will declaration executed in accordance with this act is presumed to be valid. For purposes of this act, a health care provider may presume in the absence of actual notice to the contrary that the declarant was of sound mind when it was executed. The fact that the declarant executed a declaration may not be considered as an indication of a declarant's mental incompetency.

Penalties. A person who knowingly or intentionally physically cancels or destroys a living will declaration or a life-prolonging procedures will declaration without the declarant's consent or falsifies or forges a revocation of another person's living will declaration or life-prolonging procedures will declaration commits a Class D felony. A person who knowingly or intentionally falsifies or forges the living will declaration of another person with intent to cause withholding or withdrawal of life-prolonging procedures or conceals or withholds personal knowledge of the revocation of a living will declaration with intent to cause a withholding or withdrawal of life-prolonging procedures commits a Class C felony (a person who has been found guilty, or guilty but mentally ill, of such an offense is subject to IC 29-1-2-12.1).

Suicide. A death caused by the withholding or withdrawal of life-prolonging procedures in accordance with this act does not constitute a suicide.

Insurance. The execution of a living will declaration or a life-prolonging procedures will declaration under this act does not affect the sale or issuance of any life insurance policy or modify the terms of a policy in force when the declaration is executed. A policy of life insurance is not legally impaired or invalidated by the withholding or withdrawal of life-prolonging procedures from an insured qualified patient, notwithstanding any term of the policy to the contrary.

Conditional execution of declaration. A person may not require another person to execute a living will declaration or a life-prolonging procedures will declaration as a condition for being insured for, or receiving, health care services.

Presumption of intent. This act creates no presumption concerning the intention of a person who has not executed a living will declaration to consent to the withholding or withdrawal of life-prolonging procedures in the event of a terminal condition.

Limitations. Nothing in this act shall be construed to authorize euthanasia or to authorize any affirmative or deliberate act or omission to end life other than to permit the natural process of dying, including the withholding or withdrawing of life-prolonging procedures under this act.

Intervening forces; proximate causation. The act of withholding or withdrawing life-prolonging procedures, when done pursuant to (1) a living will declaration made under this act; (2) a court order or decision of a court-appointed guardan; or (3) a good faith medical decision by the attending physician that the patient has a terminal condition; shall not be construed to be an intervening force or to affect the chain of proximate cause between the conduct of any person that placed the patient in a terminal condition and the patient's death.

Provisions of act cumulative. This act does not impair or supersede any legal right or legal responsibility that any person may have to effect the withholding or withdrawal of life-prolonging procedures in any lawful manner.

Violation by physician. A physician who knowingly violates this act is subject to disciplinary sanctions under IC 25-22.5-6-2.1 as if the physician had knowingly violated a rule adopted by the medical licensing board under IC 25-22.5-2-7.

IOWA: LIFE-SUSTAINING PROCEDURES ACT (1985)

Policy statement. The legislature finds that all adults have the fundamental right to control the decisions relating to their own medical care, including the decision to have medical or surgical means or procedures calculated to prolong their lives provided, withheld, or withdrawn. This right is subject to certain interests of society, such as the protection of human life and the preservation of ethical standards in the medical profession. The legislature further finds that the artificial prolongation of life for persons with a terminal condition may secure only a precarious and burdensome existence, while providing nothing medically necessary or beneficial to the patient. In order that the rights and intentions of persons with such conditions may be respected even after they are no longer able to participate actively in decisions concerning themselves, and to encourage communications between these patients, their families, and their physicians, the legislature declares that the laws of Iowa shall recognize the right of an adult to make a written declaration instructing the adult's physician to provide, withhold, or withdraw life-sustaining procedures or to designate another to make treatment decisions, in the event the person is diagnosed as suffering from a terminal condition.

Execution of declaration. Any competent adult, 18 years of age or older, may execute a declaration at any time directing that life-sustaining procedures be withheld or withdrawn.

When declaration operative. The declaration may be given operative effect only if the declarant's condition is determined to be terminal in the opinion of the attending physician, confirmed by another physician, and the declarant is not able to make treatment decisions.

Signing of declaration; witnesses. The declaration must be signed by the declarant or another at the declarant's direction in the presence of 2 persons who shall sign the declaration as witnesses.

Presumption of validity. An attending physician or health care provider may presume, in the absence of actual notice to the contrary, that the declaration complies with this act and is valid.

Definition of life-sustaining procedures; exclusions. This term shall apply to any medical procedure, treatment, or intervention which utilizes mechanical or artificial means to sustain, restore, or supplant a spontaneous vital function and, when applied to any patient in a terminal condition, would serve only to prolong the dying process. "Life-sustaining procedure" does not include the provision of sustenance or the administration of medication or the performance of any medical procedure deemed necessary to provide comfort care or to alleviate pain.

Notice to physicians. It is the responsibility of the declarant to provide the declarant's attending physician with the declaration.

Suggested form of declaration. See Appendix. A declaration executed pursuant to this act may, but need not be, in this form.

Revocation of declaration. A declaration may be revoked at any time and in any manner by which the declarant is able to communicate his intent to revoke, without regard to mental or physical condition. A revocation is only effective as to the attending physician upon communication to such physician by the declarant or by another to whom the revocation was communicated.

Revocation a part of medical record. The attending physician shall make the revocation a part of the declarant's medical record.

Recording determination of terminal condition. When an attending physician who has been provided with a declaration determines that the declarant is in a terminal condition, and this decision has been confirmed by another physician, the attending physician must record that determination in the declarant's medical record.

Treatment of qualified patient. A qualified patient who has signed a declaration in accordance with this act and who has been determined by the attending physician to be in a terminal condition has the right to make decisions regarding use of life-sustaining procedures as long as the patient is able to do so. If a qualified patient is not able to make such decisions, the declaration shall govern decisions regarding use of life-sustaining procedures.

Pregnancy. The declaration of a qualified patient known to the attending physician to be pregnant shall not be in effect as long as the fetus could develop to the point of live birth with continued application of life-sustaining procedures. However, the provisions of this subsection do not impair any existing rights or responsibilities that any person may have in regard to the withholding or withdrawal of life-sustaining procedures

Procedure in absence of declaration. Life-sustaining procedures may be withheld or withdrawn from a patient who is in a terminal condition and who is comatose, incompetent, or otherwise physically or mentally incapable of communication and has not made a declaration in accordance with this act if there is consultation and written agreement for the withholding or withdrawal of life-sustaining procedures between the attending physician and any of the following individuals, who shall be guided by the express or implied intentions of the patient, in the following order of priority if no individual in a prior class is reasonably available, willing, and competent to act: (a) The attorney-in-fact designated to make treatment decisions for the patient should such person be diagnosed as suffering from a terminal condition, if the designation is in writing and complies with section 633.705. (b) The guardian of the person of the patient if one has been appointed. This paragraph does not require the appointment of a guardian in order for a treatment decision to be made under this section. (c) The patient's spouse. (d) An adult child of the patient or, if the patient has more than 1 adult child, a majority of the adult children who are reasonably available for consultation. (e) A parent of the patient, or parents if both are reasonably available. (f) An adult sibling.

Witness. When a decision is made pursuant to this section to withhold or withdraw life-sustaining procedures in the absence of a patient declaration, there shall be a witness present at the time of the consultation when the decision is made.

Pregnancy. In the case of the absence of a patient declaration, the same exclusion for pregnancy as that noted above (in the case of a qualified patient who has made a declaration) shall apply.

Transfer. An attending physician who is unwilling to comply with the requirements of the sections above regarding "Recording Determination of Terminal Condition," "Treatment of Qualified Patient," or "Procedure in Absence of Declaration" shall take all reasonable steps to effect the transfer of the patient to another physician. If the policies of a health care provider likewise preclude compliance under these sections, the provider shall take all reasonable steps to effect the transfer of the patient to a facility in which the provisions of this act can be carried out.

Immunities. In the absence of actual notice of the revocation of a declaration, the following, while acting in accordance with the requirements of this act, are not subject to civil or criminal liability or guilty of unprofessional conduct: (a) A physician who causes the withholding or withdrawal of life-sustaining procedures from a qualified patient. (b) The health care provider in which such withholding or withdrawal occurs. (c) A person who participates in the withholding or withdrawal of life-sustaining procedures under the direction of or with the authorization of a physician. A physician is not subject to civil or criminal liability for actions under this act which are in accord with reasonable medical standards. Any person, institution, or facility against whom criminal or civil liability is asserted because of conduct in compliance with this act may interpose this legislative act as an absolute defense.

Penalties. Any person who willfully conceals, withholds, cancels, destroys, alters, defaces, or obliterates the declaration of another without the declarant's consent or who falsifies or forges a revocation of the declaration of another is guilty of a serious misdemeanor. Any person who falsifies or forges the declaration of another, or willfully conceals or withholds personal knowledge of or delivery of a revocation as provided in this act, with the intent to cause a withholding or withdrawal of life-sustaining procedures, is guilty of a serious misdemeanor.

Suicide. Death resulting from the withholding or withdrawal of life-sustaining procedures pursuant to a declaration and in accordance with this act does not, for any purpose, constitute a suicide or homicide.

Insurance. The making of a declaration does not affect in any manner the sale, procurement, or issuance of any policy of life insurance, nor shall it be deemed to modify the terms of an existing policy of life insurance. No policy of life insurance is legally impaired or invalidated in any manner by the withholding or withdrawal of life-sustaining procedures pursuant to this act, notwithstanding any term of the policy to the contrary.

Conditional execution of declaration. A physician, health care provider, health care service plan, insurer issuing disability insurance, self-insured employee welfare benefit plan, or nonprofit hospital plan shall not require any person to execute a declaration as a condition for being insured for, or receiving, health care services.

Presumption of intent. This act creates no presumption concerning the intention of an individual who has not executed a declaration with respect to the use, withholding, or withdrawal of life-sustaining procedures in the event of a terminal condition.

Cumulative nature of provisions. This act shall not be interpreted to increase or decrease the right of a patient to make decisions regarding use of life-sustaining procedures as long as the patient is able to do so, nor to impair or supersede any right or responsibility that any person has to effect the withholding or withdrawal of medical care in any lawful manner. In that respect, the provisions of this act are cumulative.

Mercy killing. This act shall not be construed to condone, authorize, or approve mercy killing or euthanasia, or to permit any affirmative or deliberate act or omission to end life other than to permit the natural process of dying.

KANSAS: NATURAL DEATH ACT (1979)

Legislative policy statement. The legislature finds that adult persons have the fundamental right to control the decisions relating to the rendering of their own medical care, including the decision to have life-sustaining procedures withheld or withdrawn in instances of a terminal condition. In order that the rights of patients may be respected even after they are no longer able to participate actively in decisions about themselves, the legislature hereby declares that the laws of this state shall recognize the right of an adult person to make a written declaration instructing his or her physician to withhold or withdraw life-sustaining procedures in the event of a terminal condition.

Execution of declaration. Any adult person at least 18 years of age may execute a declaration directing the withholding or withdrawal of life-sustaining procedures in a terminal condition. The declaration made pursuant to this act shall be: (1) In writing; (2) Signed by the person making the declaration, or by another person in the declarant's presence and by the declarant's expressed direction; (3) Dated; and (4) Signed in the presence of 2 or more witnesses.

Witnesses. Each witness to a declaration shall be at least 18 years of age and neither shall be the person who signed the declaration on behalf of and at the direction of the person making the declaration. Neither shall be related to the declarant by blood or marriage, entitled to any portion of the estate of the declarant according to the laws of intestate succession of this state or under any will of the declarant or codicil thereto, or directly financially responsible for declarant's medical care.

Pregnancy. The declaration of a qualified patient shall have no effect during the course of a qualified patient's pregnancy. ("Qualified patient" means a patient who has executed a declaration in accordance with this act and who has been diagnosed and certified in writing to be afflicted with a terminal condition by 2 physicians who have personally examined the patient, one of whom shall be the attending physician.)

Notification of physician. It shall be the responsibility of the declarant to provide for notification to his or her attending physician of the existence of the declaration. An attending physician who is so notified shall make the declaration, or a copy of the declaration, a part of the declarant's medical records.

Recommended form of declaration. For a copy of the suggested form of the declaration, to which the declarant may make personal additions, see Appendix.

Additional directions severable. Should any of the other specific directions added by the declarant be held to be invalid, such invalidity shall not affect other directions of the declaration which can be given effect without the invalid directions; to this end the directions in the declaration are severable.

Revocation of declaration. A declaration may be revoked at any time by the declarant by any of the following methods: (1) By being obliterated, burnt, torn, or otherwise destroyed or defaced in a manner indicating intention to cancel; (2) By a written revocation of the declaration signed and dated by the declarant or person acting at the direction of the declarant; (3) By a verbal expression of the intent to revoke the declaration, in the presence of a witness 18 years of age or older who signs and dates a writing confirming that such expression of intent was made.

Notice of revocation. Any verbal revocation shall become effective upon receipt by the attending physician of the above mentioned writing. The attending physician shall record in the patient's medical record the time, date, and place of when he or she received notification of the revocation. There shall be no criminal or civil liability on the part of any person for failure to act upon a revocation made pursuant to this section unless that person has actual knowledge of the revocation.

Written certification of terminal condition. An attending physician who has been notified of the existence of a declaration executed under this act, without delay after the diagnosis of a terminal condition of the declarant, shall take the necessary steps to provide for written certification and confirmation of the declarant's terminal condition, so that the declarant may be deemed to be a qualified patient under this act. An attending physician who fails to comply with this section shall be deemed to have refused to comply with this declaration and shall be subject to the section on "Transfer" below.

Operative effect of declaration. The desires of a qualified patient shall at all times supersede the effect of the declaration. If the qualified patient is incompetent at the time of the decision to withhold or withdraw life-sustaining procedures, a declaration executed in accordance with this act is presumed to be valid.

Presumption of validity. For the purpose of this act, a physician or medical care facility may presume in the absence of actual notice to the contrary that an individual who executed a declaration was of sound mind when it was executed. The fact of an individual's having executed a declaration shall not be considered as an indication of a declarant's mental incompetency. Age of itself shall not be a bar to a determination of competency.

Immunity. No physician, licensed health care professional, medical care facility or employee thereof who in good faith and pursuant to reasonable medical standards causes or participates in the withholding or withdrawal of life-sustaining procedures from a qualified patient who has made a declaration in accordance with this act shall, as a result thereof, be subject to criminal or civil liability, or be found to have committed an act of unprofessional conduct.

Transfer. An attending physician who refuses to comply with the declaration of a qualified patient pursuant to this act shall effect the transfer of the qualified patient to another physician. Failure of an attending physician to comply with the declaration of a qualified patient and to effect the transfer of the qualified patient shall constitute unprofessional conduct as defined in K. S. A. 65-2837.

Penalties. Any person who willfully conceals, cancels, defaces, obliterates, or damages the declaration of another without such declarant's consent or who falsifies or forges a revocation of the declaration of another shall be guilty of a class A misdemeanor. Any person who falsifies or forges the declaration of another, or willfully conceals or withholds personal knowledge of the revocation of a declaration, with the intent to cause a withholding or withdrawal of life-sustaining procedures contrary to the wishes of the declarant, and thereby, because of such act, directly causes life-sustaining procedures to be withheld or withdrawn and death to be hastened, shall be guilty of a class E felony.

Suicide. The withholding or withdrawal of life-sustaining procedures from a qualified patient in accordance with the provisions of this act shall not, for any purpose, constitute a suicide and shall not constitute the crime of assisting suicide as defined by K. S. A. 21-3406.

Insurance. The making of a declaration pursuant to this act shall not affect in any manner the sale, procurement, or issuance of any policy of life insurance, nor shall it be deemed to modify the terms of an existing policy of life insurance. No policy of life insurance shall be legally impaired or invalidated in any manner by the withholding or withdrawal of life-sustaining procedures from an insured qualified patient, notwithstanding any term of the policy to the contrary.

Conditional execution of declaration. No physician, medical care facility, or other health care provider, and no health care service plan, health maintenance organization, insurer issuing disability insurance, self-insured employee welfare benefit plan, nonprofit medical service corporation, or mutual nonprofit hospital service corporation shall require any person to execute a declaration as a condition for being insured for, or receiving, health care services.

Presumption of intent. This act shall create no presumption concerning the intention of an individual who has not executed a declaration to consent to the use or withholding of life-sustaining procedures in the event of a terminal condition.

Definition of life-sustaining procedure. The term "life-sustaining procedure" as used in this act shall not include the administration of medication or the performance of any medical procedure deemed necessary to provide comfort care or to alleviate pain.

Mercy killing. Nothing in this act shall be construed to condone, authorize, or approve mercy killing or to permit any affirmative or deliberate act or omission to end life other than to permit the natural process of dying as provided in this act.

LOUISIANA: DECLARATIONS CONCERNING LIFE-SUSTAINING PROCEDURES ACT (1984; amended 1985)

Legislative purpose and findings. The legislature finds that all persons have the fundamental right to control the decisions relating to their own medical care, including the decision to have life-sustaining procedures withheld or withdrawn in instances where such persons are diagnosed as having a terminal and irreversible condition. The legislature further finds that the artificial prolongation of life for a person diagnosed as having a terminal and irreversible condition may cause loss of individual and personal dignity and secure only a precarious and burdensome existence while providing nothing medically necessary or beneficial to the person. In order that the rights of such persons may be respected even after they are no longer able to participate actively in decisions concerning themselves, the legislature hereby declares that the laws of the state of Louisiana shall recognize: (a) The right of such a person to make a declaration instructing his physician to withhold or withdraw life-sustaining procedures or designating another to make the treatment decision and make such a declaration for him, in the event he is diagnosed as having a terminal and irreversible condition; and (b) The right of certain individuals to make a declaration pursuant to which life-sustaining procedures may be withheld or withdrawn from an adult patient who is comatose, incompetent, or otherwise physically or mentally incapable of communication, or from a minor, in the event such adult patient or minor is diagnosed and certified as having a terminal and irreversible condition. In furtherance of the rights of such persons, the legislature finds and declares that nothing in this act shall be construed to be the exclusive means by which life-sustaining procedures may be withheld or withdrawn, nor shall this act be construed to require the application of medically inappropriate treatment or life-sustaining procedures to any patient or to interfere with medical judgment with respect to the application of medical treatment or life-sustaining procedures.

Legislative intent. The legislature intends that the provisions of this act are permissive and voluntary. The legislature further intends that the making of a declaration pursuant to this act merely illustrates a means of documenting a patient's decision relative to withholding or withdrawal of medical treatment or life-sustaining procedures. It is the intent of the legislature that nothing in this act shall be construed to require the making of a declaration pursuant to this act. It is the intent of the legislature that nothing in this act shall be construed to be the exclusive means by which life-sustaining procedures may be withheld or withdrawn, nor shall this act be construed to require the application of medically inappropriate treatment or life-sustaining procedures to any patient or to interfere with medical judgment with respect to the application of medical treatment or life-sustaining procedures.

Making of declaration. A declaration may be made in writing, orally, or by other means of nonverbal communication. Any adult person may, at any time, make a written declaration directing the withholding or withdrawal of life-sustaining procedures in the event such person should have a terminal and medically irreversible condition.

Witnesses. A written declaration shall be signed by the declarant in the presence of 2 witnesses, who are competent adults and not related to the declarant by blood or marriage and would not be entitled to any portion of the estate of the person from whom life-sustaining procedures are to be withheld or withdrawn upon his decease. An oral or nonverbal declaration may be made by an adult in the presence of 2 witnesses by any nonwritten means of communication at any time subsequent to the diagnosis of a terminal and irreversible condition.

Notification. It shall be the responsibility of the declarant to notify his attending physician that a declaration has been made. In the event the declarant is comatose, incompetent, or otherwise mentally or physically incapable of communication, any other person may notify the physician of the existence of the declaration.

Entry in medical record. Any attending physician who is so notified shall promptly make the declaration or copy of the declaration, if written, a part of the declarant's medical record. If the declaration is oral or nonverbal, the physician shall promptly make a recitation of the reasons the declarant could not make a written declaration and make the recitation a part of the patient's medical records.

Recommended form of declaration. See Appendix. The declaration may, but need not be, in this illustrative form and may include other specific directions including but not limited to a designation of another person to make the treatment decision for the declarant should he be diagnosed as having a terminal and irreversible condition and be comatose, incompetent, or otherwise mentally or physically incapable of communications.

Definition of life-sustaining procedure; excluded treatment. A "life-sustaining procedure" shall not include any measure deemed necessary to provide comfort care.

Revocation. A declaration may be revoked at any time by the declarant without regard to his or her mental state or competency by any of the following methods: (1) By being cancelled, defaced, obliterated, burned, torn, or otherwise destroyed by the declarant or by some person in the presence of and at the direction of the declarant. (2) By a written revocation of the declarant expressing the intent to revoke, signed and dated by the declarant. (3) By an oral or nonverbal expression by the declarant of the intent to revoke the declaration.

Revocation effective; entry in medical record. Revocation by any method enumerated in the above section shall become effective upon communication to the attending physician. The attending physician shall record in the patient's medical records the time and date when notification of the revocation was received.

Procedure for making a declaration for a patient diagnosed and certified in writing as having a terminal and irreversible condition who has not previously made a declaration. Nothing in this act shall be construed in any manner to prevent the withholding or the withdrawal of life-sustaining procedures from a qualified patient with a terminal and irreversible condition who is comatose, incompetent, or otherwise physically or mentally incapable of communication and has not made a prior declaration in accordance with this act. ("Qualified patient" means a patient diagnosed and certified in writing as having a terminal and irreversible condition by 2 physicians who have personally examined the patient, one of whom shall be the attending physician.) When a comatose or incompetent person or a person who is physically or mentally incapable of communication has been certified as a qualified patient and has not previously made a declaration, any of the following individuals in the following order of priority, if there is no individual in a prior class who is reasonably available, willing, and competent to act, may make a declaration on the qualified patient's behalf: (a) The judicially appointed tutor or curator of the patient if one has been appointed (this subparagraph shall not be construed to require such appointment in order that a declaration can be made under this section). (b) The patient's spouse not judicially separated. (c) An adult child of the patient. (d) The parents of the patient. (e) The patient's sibling. (f) The patient's other ascendants or descendants. If there is more than one person within the above named class in subparagraphs (c) through (f), then the declaration shall be made by all of that class available for consultation upon good faith efforts to secure participation of all of that class. In any case where the declaration is made by a person specified in subparagraphs (b), (c), (d), (e), or (f), there shall be at least 2 witnesses present at the time the declaration is made.

Presumption as to intent. The absence of a declaration by an adult patient shall not give rise to any presumption as to the intent to consent to or to refuse life-sustaining procedures.

Making a declaration for the benefit of a terminally ill minor. If a minor has been certified as a qualified patient having a terminal condition, the following individuals may voluntarily make a declaration to document the decision relative to withholding or withdrawal of medical treatment or life-sustaining procedures on a minor's behalf: (1) The spouse if he or she has reached the age of majority; or (2) If there is no spouse, or if the spouse is not available, or is a minor, or is otherwise unable to act, then either the parent or guardian of the minor. An individual named in subsections (1) or (2) may not make a declaration if he has actual notice of contrary indications by the minor who is terminally ill or if, as a parent or guardian, he has actual notice of opposition by either another parent, or guardian, or a spouse who has attained the age of majority.

Provisions permissive and voluntary. Nothing in the previous section shall be construed to require the making of a declaration for a terminally ill minor. The legislature intends that the provisions of this act are permissive and voluntary. The legislature further intends that the making of a declaration pursuant to this act merely illustrates a means of documenting the decision relative to withholding or withdrawal of medical treatment or life-sustaining procedures on behalf of a minor.

Physician responsibility; transfer. Any attending physician who has been notified of the existence of a declaration made under this act or at the request of the proper person, as provided in the case of qualified patients with a terminal condition who have not made a declaration, upon diagnosis of a terminal and irreversible condition of the patient, shall take necessary steps to provide for written certification of the patient's terminal and irreversible condition, so that the patient may be deemed to be a qualified patient. Any attending physician who refuses to comply with the declaration of a qualified patient or declaration otherwise made pursuant to this act shall make a reasonable effort to transfer the patient to another physician.

Immunity from liability. Any health care facility, physician, or other person acting under the direction of a physician shall not be subject to criminal prosecution or civil liability or be deemed to have engaged in unprofessional conduct as a result of authorizing or effectuating the withholding or withdrawing of life-sustaining procedures from a qualified patient with a terminal and irreversible condition in accordance with the provisions of this act, or in accordance with provisions other than those enumerated in this act used to document or manifest the patient's or his representative's intention and desire that medical treatment or life-sustaining procedures be withheld or withdrawn when such continued utilization of life-sustaining procedures would, within reasonable medical judgment, serve only to prolong the dying process. Inasmuch as the provisions of this act are declared by the legislature to provide an alternative nonexclusive means by which life-sustaining procedures may be withheld or withdrawn, the provisions of this section shall apply to any case in which life-sustaining procedures are withheld or withdrawn unless it is shown by a preponderance of the evidence that the person authorizing or effectuating the withholding or withdrawal of life-sustaining procedures did not, in good faith, comply with the provisions of this act or did not act in good faith compliance with the intention of the terminal and irreversible patient that medical treatment or life-sustaining procedures be withheld or withdrawn. A declaration made in accordance with this act shall be presumed to have been made voluntarily.

Penalties. Any person who willfully conceals, cancels, defaces, obliterates, or damages the declaration of another without such declarant's consent or who falsifies or forges a revocation of the declaration of another shall be civilly liable. Any person who falsifies or forges the declaration of another or willfully conceals or withholds personal knowledge of a revocation of a declaration with the intent to cause the withholding or withdrawal of life-sustaining procedures contrary to the wishes of the declarant, and thereby because of such act directly causes life-sustaining procedures to be withheld or withdrawn and death thereby to be hastened may be subject to prosecution under Title 14 of the Louisiana Revised Statutes of 1950.

Mercy killing. Nothing in this act shall be construed to condone, authorize, or approve mercy killing or euthanasia or to permit any affirmative or deliberate act or omission to end life other than to permit the natural process of dying.

Suicide. The withholding or withdrawal of life-sustaining procedures from a qualified patient in accordance with the provisions of this act shall not, for any purpose, constitute a suicide.

Life insurance. The making of a declaration pursuant to this act shall not affect the sale, procurement, or issuance of any life insurance policy, nor shall it be deemed to modify the terms of an existing policy. No policy shall be legally impaired or invalidated by the withholding or withdrawal of life-sustaining procedures from an insured, qualified patient, notwithstanding any term of the policy to the contrary. The removal of life support systems under this act shall not be deemed the cause of death for purposes of insurance coverage.

Conditional execution of declaration. A person shall not be required to make a declaration as a condition for being insured or for receiving health care services.

Cumulative effects. The provisions of this act are cumulative with existing law pertaining to an individual's right to consent or refuse to consent to medical or surgical treatment.

MAINE: LIVING WILL ACT (1985)

Execution of declaration. A competent individual 18 years of age or older may execute a declaration at any time directing that life-sustaining procedures be withheld or withdrawn. The declaration must be signed by the declarant, or another at the declarant's direction, in the presence of 2 subscribing witnesses.

Incorporation in medical record. A physician or other health care provider who is provided a copy of the declaration shall make it a part of the declarant's medical record.

Operative effect. A declaration has operative effect only when the declaration is communicated to the attending physician, the declarant is determined by the attending physician to be in a terminal condition, and the declarant is unable to make treatment decisions.

Recommended form of declaration. For the suggested form which the declaration may, but does not have to, follow, see Appendix.

Revocation. A declaration may be revoked at any time and in any manner by which the declarant is able to communicate an intent to revoke, without regard to mental or physical condition. A revocation is only effective as to the attending physician or any health care provider upon communication to the physician by the declarant or by another who witnessed the communication of the intent to revoke.

Revocation part of medical record. The attending physician or health care provider shall make the revocation a part of the declarant's medical record.

Recording determination of terminal condition and contents of declaration.

Upon determining that the declarant is in a terminal condition, the attending physician who has been notified of the existence and contents of a declaration shall record the determination and the substance of the declaration in the declarant's medical record.

Decisions regarding the use of life-sustaining procedures. A patient who has executed a declaration has the right to make decisions regarding use of life-sustaining procedures as long as the patient is able to do so. If a patient is not able to make these decisions, the declaration shall govern decisions regarding use of life-sustaining procedures.

Comfort care; alleviation of pain. This act does not prohibit any action considered necessary by the attending physician to provide for comfort care or the alleviation of pain.

Definition of life-sustaining procedure; excluded treatments. "Life-sustaining procedure" means any medical procedure or intervention that will serve only to prolong the dying process and shall not include nutrition and hydration.

Transfer of patients. An attending physician or health care provider who is unwilling to comply with this act shall take all reasonable steps to effect the transfer of the declarant to another physician or health care provider in order to comply with this act.

Immunities. In the absence of actual notice of the revocation of a declaration, a physician who causes the withholding or withdrawal of life-sustaining procedures from a qualified patient who has executed a declaration and a person who participates in the withholding or withdrawal of life-sustaining procedures under the direction or authorization of the physician, while acting in accordance with the requirements of this act, are not subject to civil or criminal liability or charges of unprofessional conduct.

Penalty for willful failure to transfer. A physician or health care provider who willfully fails to transfer in accordance with the above subsection on "Transfer of patients" is guilty of a Class E crime.

Failure to record determination of terminal condition. A physician who willfully fails to record the determination of a terminal condition is guilty of a Class E crime.

Concealing, canceling, defacing, or obliterating declaration. Any person who willfully conceals, cancels, defaces, or obliterates the declaration of another without the declarant's consent or who falsifies or forges a revocation of the declaration of another is guilty of a Class E crime.

Falsification or forgery of declaration. Any person who falsifies or forges the declaration of another or willfully conceals or withholds personal knowledge of a revocation as provided in the subsection of this act on "Revocation," with the intent to cause a withholding or withdrawal of life-sustaining procedures, is guilty of a Class B crime.

Death not suicide or homicide. Death resulting from the withholding or withdrawal of life-sustaining procedures pursuant to a declaration and in accordance with this act does not, for any purpose, constitute a suicide or homicide.

Declaration not to affect insurance. The making of a declaration relating to the use of life-sustaining procedures does not affect in any manner the sale, procurement, or issuance of any policy of life insurance, nor is it deemed to modify the terms of an existing policy of life insurance. A policy of life insurance is not legally impaired or invalidated in any manner by the withholding or withdrawal of life-sustaining procedures from an insured patient who has executed a declaration, notwithstanding any term of the policy to the contrary.

Conditional execution of declaration. A person may not prohibit or require the execution of a declaration by any individual as a condition for being insured for or receiving health care services.

Presumption concerning life-sustaining procedures. This act creates no presumption concerning the intention of an individual who has not executed or who has revoked a declaration with respect to the use, withholding, or withdrawal of life-sustaining procedures in the event of a terminal condition.

Patient's right. Nothing in this act may be interpreted to increase or decrease the right of a patient to make decisions regarding use of life-sustaining procedures as long as the patient is able to do so, or to impair or supersede any right or responsibility that any person has to effect the withholding or withdrawal of medical care in any lawful manner. In that respect, the provisions of this act are cumulative.

Mercy killing. This act does not condone, authorize, or approve mercy killing, euthanasia, or suicide.

Recognition of declaration executed in other states. A declaration executed in another state in compliance with the laws of that state or this state is validly executed for purposes of this act.

Presumption of validity. A physician or health care provider may presume in the absence of actual notice to the contrary that a declaration executed in this state or another state complies with this act and is valid.

MARYLAND: LIFE-SUSTAINING PROCEDURES ACT (1985)

Requirements. Any individual qualified to make a will under the laws of Maryland may execute a declaration, directing the withholding or withdrawal of life-sustaining procedures. The declaration shall be (1) Voluntary; (2) Dated and in writing; (3) Signed by the declarant or, if at the declarant's expressed direction and in the declarant's presence, by another individual on behalf of the declarant; (4) Executed in the presence of and attested by at least 2 witnesses.

Qualifications of witnesses. Each witness must be at least 18 years old. A witness may not be (a) An individual who signed the declaration at the direction and on behalf of the declarant, as provided under subsection (3) above; (b) Related to the declarant by blood or marriage within a degree listed under section 2-202 of the Family Law Article; (c) Either a creditor of the declarant or knowingly entitled to any portion of the estate of the declarant under the provisions of the declarant's last will and testament or knowingly entitled to any other financial interest deriving from the declarant; or (d) Financially or otherwise responsible for the declarant's medical care or an employee of any such person.

Notice to physician. A declarant is responsible for notifying the attending physician of the existence of the declaration either directly or through another individual. Notice may be given by delivery of the declaration or a copy of the declaration to the attending physician. The attending physician shall make the declaration or other written documents containing a declaration a part of the declarant's medical records.

Recommended form of declaration. See Appendix. The declaration shall be substantially in the form provided. In addition, it may include other provisions on this or other subjects that are not inconsistent with other provisions of this act.

Additional provisions severable. If any additional provisions added to the declaration are declared invalid, the invalidity does not affect the validity of the declaration or of other provisions which can be given effect without the invalid provision; to this end the provisions in the declaration are severable.

Definition of life-sustaining procedure. "Life-sustaining procedure" means any medical procedure, treatment, or intervention which uses mechanical or other artificial means to sustain, restore, or supplant a spontaneous vital function. (In the model Declaration provided in this act, the administration of food and water is specifically excluded, however, from the medical treatments that are permitted to be withheld or withdrawn and is specifically forbidden in the section on "Other Exceptions When Declaration May Not be Implemented" below.)

Revocation. A declarant may revoke a declaration at any time by: (1) A written statement to that effect, either signed and dated by the declarant or, if the statement so indicates, signed and dated by a person acting at the direction of the declarant; (2) An expression to that effect, after the declarant knows of the disease, illness, or injury involved in any question regarding the existence of a terminal condition; (3) Destroying the declaration; (4) Marking, burning, tearing, or otherwise altering, defacing, or damaging the declaration in a manner indicating the intention to revoke it.

When declaration operative. If the declarant is unable to give directions regarding the use of life-sustaining procedures, the attending physician of a declarant in a terminal condition shall promptly take the steps necessary to provide for the certification required for the declaration to become operative; upon certification in writing of the patient's terminal condition, after an examination by 2 physicians, at least one of whom is an attending physician of the declarant, the patient shall be certified to be a "qualified patient" and the declaration shall be implemented.

Transfer of patient. An attending physician who does not comply with this certification and implementation procedure shall make every reasonable effort to transfer the declarant to another physician.

Revoked declaration. If the attending physician knows that the declaration has been revoked or for so long as the physician has a reasonable basis for believing that the declaration may have been revoked, the declaration shall not be implemented.

Basis for physician's conclusion placed in medical records. The attending physician shall place in the declarant's medical records the evidentiary basis for the physician's conclusion: (1) That a valid and unrevoked declaration exists, if the physician certifies and implements the declaration; or (2) That the declaration has been revoked or may have been revoked if the physician acts under the section titled "Revoked Declaration" above.

Other exceptions when declaration may not be implemented. The declaration of a qualified patient to withhold or withdraw life-sustaining procedures may not be implemented: (1) By the denial of food, water, or of such medication and medical procedures as are necessary to provide comfort care and to alleviate pain; or (2) If the qualified patient is pregnant.

Declaration presumed valid. In the absence of evidence to the contrary, a declaration which, on its face, satisfies the requirements of this act is presumed to be valid.

Civil liability. Excluding the exceptions noted in the following section, on notification of the existence of a valid declaration any person who causes a failure to comply with the certification and implementation of the declaration may be held civilly liable.

Certain health care providers not liable. A paid or volunteer fire fighter, paramedic, or member of an ambulance or rescue squad is not subject to criminal or civil liability for aid, care, or assistance rendered in good faith and under reasonable standards to a qualified patient, even if that aid, care, or assistance is contrary to the provisions of the qualified patient's declaration.

Liability of nonprofessionals. A person who in good faith, pursuant to reasonable medical standards, and in accordance with the requirements of this act, causes or participates in the withholding or withdrawal of life-sustaining procedures from a qualified patient is not subject to civil or criminal liability and may not have been found to have committed professional misconduct. This immunity from liability does not apply to any acts or omissions prior to the time a declarant becomes a qualified patient or exempt any person from liability or professional responsibility for willful or wanton misconduct or for negligence.

Conditional execution of declaration. A person or other legal entity may not require execution of a declaration as a condition for providing shelter, insurance coverage, or health care benefits or services.

Prohibited actions by life insurers. A life insurer, as defined in Article 48A of the Code, because of the execution or implementation of a declaration under this act, may not decline to provide or continue coverage to the declarant; consider the terms of an existing policy of life insurance to have been breached or modified; or invoke any suicide or intentional death exemption or exclusion in any policy covering the declarant.

Provisions cumulative. The provisions of this act are cumulative and may not be construed to impair or supersede any legal right or responsibility that any person may have to effect the initiation, continuation, withholding, or withdrawal of life-sustaining procedures.

Presumption of intent. The provisions of this act do not create a presumption concerning the intention of an individual who is in a terminal condition and who has not executed a declaration regarding the initiation, continuation, withholding, or withdrawal of life-sustaining procedures.

Mercy killing. The provisions of this act may not be construed to permit any affirmative or deliberate act or omission to end life other than to permit the withholding or withdrawing of life-sustaining procedures from a declarant in a terminal condition.

Declaration for initiation or continuation of life-sustaining procedures. An individual who is qualified to make a will under Maryland law, in place of a declaration authorizing the withholding or withdrawal of life-sustaining procedures, may execute a declaration directing the initiation or continuation of life-sustaining procedures in accordance with standard medical practice.

Execution of more than one declaration. If an individual validly executes more than 1 declaration under this act, only the last executed declaration shall be given effect.

Declarations executed outside the state. A declaration executed outside of Maryland by a nonresident shall be given effect in this state if that declaration is in compliance with the provisions of this act.

Suicide. An act authorized by this law may not, for any purpose, be considered to be a suicide or a violation of any criminal law or standard of professional conduct.

Forgeries. Any person who forges a revocation or a declaration, or who willfully purports by any other method to revoke a declaration without the consent of the declarant, or who willfully conceals or withholds personal knowledge of a revocation is guilty of a misdemeanor and on conviction is subject to a fine not exceeding $1,000.

MISSISSIPPI: WITHDRAWAL OF LIFE-SAVING MECHANISMS ACT (1984)

Legislative purpose. The purpose of this act is to allow a person to authorize the withdrawal of life-sustaining mechanisms from his body under the conditions provided by this act.

Age requirement; mental competency. Any person of the age of 18 years or older who is mentally competent may authorize withdrawal of life-sustaining mechanisms.

Pregnancy. A declaration authorizing withdrawal of life-sustaining mechanisms made by an individual diagnosed as pregnant shall have no force or effect during the course of the individual's pregnancy.

Recommended form of declaration. See the Appendix for the model form for Mississippi, which the declaration shall "substantially" follow.

Definition. "Withdrawal of life-sustaining mechanisms" shall mean the cessation of use of extraordinary techniques and applications, including mechanical devices, which prolong life through artificial means (nutrition and hydration not specifically excluded).

Filing. The declaration shall be filed with the Bureau of Vital Statistics of the State Board of Health.

Revocation. A declaration authorizing withdrawal of life-sustaining mechanisms may be revoked by a revocation signed by the declarant and at least 2 persons who witnessed the declarant's execution of the revocation.

Recommended form of revocation. See Appendix. The revocation shall be "substantially" in this form.

Filing. The revocation shall be filed with the Bureau of Vital Statistics of the State Board of Health.

Oral revocation. If a declarant wishes to revoke the authorization for withdrawal of life-sustaining mechanisms but is unable physically to execute a written revocation, a clear expression by the declarant, oral or otherwise, of the wish to revoke the authorization is effective as a revocation of authorization.

Physician's determination final. An attending physician having actual knowledge or reason to believe that his patient has executed a declaration in conformance with this act may ask the declarant, prior to procedures which might reasonably be expected to cause the declarant to become permanently unconscious or unable to make his wishes known, if said declarant revokes his declaration. The physician's determination of declarant's response in such situations shall be final.

Signature of declarant or maker of revocation; witnesses. A declaration and a revocation, except for the type of oral revocation provided by the section on "Oral Revocation" above, are valid only if signed by the declarant or maker of the revocation in the presence of at least 2 attesting witnesses who, at the time the declaration or revocation is executed, are not: (a) Related to the declarant or maker of the revocation by blood or marriage; or (b) Entitled to any portion of the estate of the declarant or maker of the revocation upon his decease under any will or codicil of the declarant or maker of the revocation or by operation of law at the time of the execution of the declaration or revocation; or (c) The attending physician or an employee of the attending physician or of a health facility in which the declarant or maker of the revocation is a patient; or (d) Persons who at the time of the execution of the declaration or revocation have a claim against any portion of the estate of the declarant or maker of the revocation upon the death of the declarant or maker of the revocation.

Withdrawal of life-sustaining mechanisms. A declaration executed and filed in the manner required by this act shall be honored when the declarant suffers a terminal physical condition causing severe distress or unconsciousness and the declarant's physician and 2 other physicians concur that there is no expectation that the declarant will regain consciousness or a state of health that is meaningful to the declarant and that but for the use of life-sustaining mechanisms the declarant would immediately die.

Verification of declaration by physician. Before withdrawing life-sustaining mechanisms from a patient, the physician in charge must be satisfied that the patient has authorized the action as provided in this act, and, in particular, such physician shall request and receive a certified copy of the declaration and a certificate that no revocation has been filed of record with the Bureau of Vital Statistics of the State Board of Health.

Transfer of patient to another physician or facility. No physician or medical facility has a duty to participate in the withdrawal of life-sustaining mechanisms authorized by this act, but a physician or medical facility not honoring a patient's authorization has a duty to cooperate in the transfer of the patient to another physician or medical facility that will give effect to such an authorization made in accordance with this act.

Transplants. No physician participating in a decision to withdraw life-sustaining mechanisms from a declarant may participate in transplanting the vital organs of the declarant to another person.

Exemption of physician from criminal prosecution or civil liability. A physician who in good faith and in accordance with the provisions of this act causes withdrawal of life-sustaining mechanisms is not guilty of a criminal offense or subject to civil liability for his action and is not in breach of a professional oath, affirmation, or standard of care.

Mercy killing. Nothing in this act shall be construed to condone, authorize, or approve the taking of life for merciful reasons, or to permit any affirmative or deliberate action or omission to end life other than to permit the natural process of dying as provided in this act.

Suicide. The authorization of withdrawal of life-sustaining mechanisms under the provisions of this act may not for any purpose be considered suicide.

Life insurance. An authorization of withdrawal of life-sustaining mechanisms or the actual withdrawal of life-sustaining mechanisms made or performed under the provisions of this act may not modify in any manner the terms of a life insurance policy nor shall it restrict, inhibit, or impair in any manner the sale, procurement, or issuance of any life insurance policy. No provision of a life insurance policy purporting to restrict, limit, negate, or alter in any manner the benefits, conditions, or terms of the policy on account of an authorization of withdrawal of life-sustaining mechanisms or the actual withdrawal of life-sustaining mechanisms under the provisions of this act is valid.

<u>Conditional execution of declaration.</u> No physician, medical facility, or other health provider, and no health care service plan, insurer issuing disability insurance, self-insured employee welfare benefit plan, or nonprofit hospital service plan shall require any person to execute a declaration or revocation pursuant to this act as a condition for being insured for, or receiving, health care service.

<u>Criminal offenses.</u> Any person who falsifies or forces the declaration of another, or willfully conceals or withholds personal knowledge of a revocation as provided in this act, with the intent to cause a withholding or withdrawal of life-sustaining procedures contrary to the wishes of the declarant, and thereby, because of any such act, directly causes life-sustaining procedures to be withheld or withdrawn and death to thereby be hastened, shall be guilty of a felony and upon conviction shall be sentenced to the custody of the Department of Corrections for not more than 20 years.

MISSOURI: UNIFORM RIGHTS OF THE TERMINALLY ILL ACT (1985)

<u>Who may execute requirements of declaration.</u> Any competent person 18 years of age or older of sound mind who is able to receive and evaluate information and to communicate a decision may execute a declaration directing the withholding or withdrawal of death-prolonging procedures.

<u>Declaration to be in writing, signed, dated, witnessed.</u> The declaration shall be (1) In writing; (2) Signed by the person making the declaration, or by another person in the declarant's presence and by the declarant's expressed direction; (3) Dated; and (4) If not wholly in the declarant's handwriting, signed in the presence of 2 or more witnesses at least 18 years of age, neither of whom shall be the person who signed the declaration on behalf of and at the direction of the person making the declaration.

<u>Notice to physician.</u> It shall be the responsibility of the declarant to provide for notification to his attending physician of the existence of the declaration. Upon the request of the patient, the declaration shall be placed in the declarant's medical records as maintained by his attending physician and the medical records of any health facility of which he is a patient.

<u>Suggested form of declaration.</u> See Appendix. The declaration may be in this form, although it shall not be necessary to use this sample form. In addition, the declaration may include other specific directions.

<u>Additional provisions severable.</u> Should any of the other specific directions be held to be invalid, such invalidity shall not affect other directions of the declaration which can be given effect without the invalid declaration, and to this end the directions in the declaration are severable.

<u>Definition of death-prolonging procedure; excluded treatments.</u> "Death-prolonging procedure" shall not include the administration of medication or the performance of medical procedure deemed necessary to provide comfort care or to alleviate pain nor the performance of any procedure to provide nutrition or

hydration.

Revocation. A declaration may be revoked at any time and in any manner by which the declarant is able to communicate his intent to revoke, without regard to physical or mental condition. The attending physician or health care provider shall make the revocation a part of the declarant's medical record. There shall be no criminal or civil liability on the part of any person for failure to act upon a revocation made pursuant to this act unless the revocation is in the patient's medical record or unless that person has actual knowledge of the revocation.

Declaration operative, when. The directions of a declarant able to make treatment decisions shall at all times supersede the declaration. The declaration shall be given operative effect only if the declarant's condition is determined to be terminal by the attending physician and the declarant is not able to make treatment decisions. Such determinations shall be recorded in the declarant's medical record. A physician, health care professional, or facility or other person shall not act contrary to the declarant's expressed intent to withhold or withdraw death-prolonging procedures without serious reason therefor consistent with the best interest of the declarant. Such reason shall be recorded in the declarant's medical record.

Pregnancy. The declaration to withhold or withdraw treatment by a patient diagnosed as pregnant shall have no effect during the course of the declarant's pregnancy.

Transfer in the case of noncompliant physician or health facility. An attending physician who is unwilling to comply with the declaration of a patient in accordance with the requirements of the above sections shall take all reasonable steps to transfer the declarant to another physician. If the policies of a health care facility preclude compliance with the declaration of a patient under this act, that facility shall take all reasonable steps to effect the transfer of the declarant to a facility in which the provisions of this act can be carried out.

Presumption of competency. For the purpose of this act, a physician or medical care facility may presume in the absence of actual notice to the contrary than an individual who executed a declaration was competent when it was executed. The fact of an individual's having executed a declaration shall not be considered as an indication of a declarant's mental incapacity. Advanced age of itself shall not be a bar to a determination of capacity.

Exemption from liability. A physician, licensed health care professional, medical care facility or employee thereof, or other person who, in good faith and pursuant to usual and customary medical standards, causes or participates in the withholding or withdrawal of death-prolonging procedures, which acts are not otherwise unlawful, from a patient pursuant to a declaration made in accordance with this act, shall not, as a result thereof, be subject to criminal or civil liability or be found to have committed an act of unprofessional conduct.

Unprofessional conduct by physician. It shall constitute unprofessional conduct if a physician or other licensed health care professional or facility with actual knowledge of a declaration acts, when the declarant is in a terminal condition and unable to make treatment decisions, contrary to the expressed intention of the declarant as stated in his declaration, without serious reason thereof consistent with the best interest of the declarant.

Inheritance rights forfeited. Any person with actual knowledge of a declaration who acts, when the declarant is in a terminal condition and unable to make treatment decisions, contrary to the expressed intention of the patient as stated in his declaration, without serious reason thereof consistent with the best interests of the patient, shall lose such rights of inheritance to the extent such loss is provided for by the patient's last will and testament.

Penalties for destroying or forging declaration. Any person who willfully conceals, cancels, defaces, obliterates, or destroys the declaration of another without such declarant's consent or who falsifies or forges a revocation of the declaration of another shall be guilty of a class A misdemeanor. Any person who falsifies or forges the declaration of another, or who willfully conceals or withholds personal knowledge of the revocation of a declaration, with the purpose of causing withholding or withdrawal of medical procedures contrary to the wishes of the declarant, and thereby, because of such act, directly causes medical procedures to be withheld or withdrawn, causing death or causing death to be hastened, shall be guilty of a class B felony.

Life insurance. The making of a declaration pursuant to this act shall not affect in any manner the sale, procurement, or issuance of any policy of life insurance, nor shall it be deemed to modify the terms of an existing policy of life insurance. No policy of life insurance shall be legally impaired or invalidated in any manner by the withholding or withdrawal of death-prolonging procedures from an insured declarant, notwithstanding any terms of the policy to the contrary.

Conditional execution of declaration. No person, corporation, or governmental agency shall require or induce any person to execute a declaration as a condition for a contract or for the provision of any service or benefit whatsoever.

Statement of purposes of declaration. The tenets of this act shall be interpreted consistent with the following: (1) Each person has the primary right to request or refuse medical treatment subject to the state's interest in protecting innocent third parties, preventing homicide and suicide, and preserving good ethical standards in the medical profession; (2) Nothing in this act shall be interpreted to increase or decrease the right of a patient to make decisions regarding use of medical procedures so long as the patient is able to do so, nor to impair or supersede any right or responsibility that any person has to effect the withholding or withdrawal of medical care in any lawful manner. In that respect, the provisions of this act are cumulative; (3) This act shall create no presumption concerning the intention of an individual who has not executed a declaration to consent to the use or withholding of medical procedures; (4) Communication regarding treatment decisions among patients, the families, and physicians is encouraged; (5) This act does not condone, authorize, or approve mercy killing or euthanasia nor permit any affirmative or deliberate act or omission to shorten or end life.

MONTANA: LIVING WILL ACT (1985)

Eligibility to execute a declaration. Any competent adult may execute a declaration at any time directing that life-sustaining procedures be withheld or withdrawn.

Declaration to be signed, witnessed. The declaration must be in writing and signed by the declarant, or another at the declarant's direction, in the presence of 2 witnesses.

When declaration is operative. The declaration is effective only if the declarant's condition is determined to be terminal and the declarant is not able to make treatment decisions.

Presumption of validity. A physician or health care provider may presume, in the absence of actual notice to the contrary, that the declaration complies with this legislative act and is valid.

Notification of physician. It is the responsibility of the declarant to notify his physician of the declaration. A physician or other health care provider who is given a copy of the declaration shall make it a part of the declarant's medical records.

Suggested form of declaration. See Appendix for the form given in the Montana statutes; the declaration may, but need not be, in this form.

Revocation of declaration. A declaration may be revoked at any time and in any manner by which the declarant is able to communicate his intent to revoke, without regard to mental or physical condition. A revocation is effective only as to the attending physician or any health care provider acting under the guidance of that physician upon communication to the physician or health care provider by the declarant or by another to whom the revocation is communicated. The attending physician or health care provider shall make the revocation a part of the declarant's medical record.

Recognition of declarations executed in other states. A declaration executed in a manner substantially similar to that of Montana in another state and in compliance with the law of that state is effective for purposes of this act.

Recording determination of terminal condition. When an attending physician who has been notified of the existence and content of a declaration determines that the declarant is in a terminal condition, the physician shall record that determination and the content of the declaration in the declarant's medical record.

Treatment of qualified patients. A qualified patient, that is, one who has executed a declaration and has been determined by the attending physician to be in a terminal condition, has the right to make decisions regarding use of life-sustaining procedures if the patient is able to do so. If a qualified patient is not able to make such decisions, the declaration governs decisions regarding the use of life-sustaining procedures.

Non-excluded treatments. This act does not prohibit the application of any medical procedure or intervention, including the provision of nutrition and hydration, considered necessary to provide comfort care or alleviate pain.

Pregnancy. The declaration of a qualified patient known to the attending physician to be pregnant must be given no effect if it is probable that the fetus could develop to the point of live birth with continued application of life-sustaining procedures.

Transfer of patients. An attending physician unwilling to comply with the declaration of a qualified patient under the terms specified above shall take all reasonable steps to transfer the declarant to another physician. If the policies of a health care facility preclude compliance with the declaration of a qualified patient under this act, that facility shall take all reasonable steps to transfer the patient to a facility in which the provisions of this act can be carried out.

Immunities. In the absence of actual notice of the revocation of a declaration, the following, while acting in accordance with the requirements of this act, are not subject to civil or criminal liability or guilty of unprofessional conduct: (a) A physician who causes the withholding or withdrawal of life-sustaining procedures from a qualified patient; (b) A person who participates in the withholding or withdrawal of life-sustaining procedures under the direction or with the authorization of a physician; (c) The health care facility in which the withholding or withdrawal occurs. A physician is not subject to civil or criminal liability for actions under this act that are in accord with reasonable medical standards.

Effect on insurance. Death resulting from the withholding or withdrawal of life-sustaining procedures pursuant to a declaration and in accordance with this act is not, for any purposes, a suicide or homicide. The making of a declaration authorizing the withholding or withdrawal of life-sustaining procedures does not affect in any manner the sale, procurement, or issuance of any policy of life insurance, nor does it modify the terms of an existing policy of life insurance. No policy of life insurance is legally impaired or invalidated in any manner by the withholding or withdrawal of life-sustaining procedures from an insured qualified patient, notwithstanding any term of the policy to the contrary.

Conditional execution of declaration. No physician, health care facility, or other health care provider, and no health care service plan, insurer issuing disability insurance, self-insured employee welfare benefit plan, or nonprofit hospital plan may require any person to execute a declaration as a condition for being insured for or receiving health care services.

Other provisions. This act creates no presumption concerning the intention of an individual who has not executed a declaration with respect to the use, withholding, or withdrawal of life-sustaining procedures in the event of a terminal condition. Nothing in this act increases or decreases the right of a patient to make decisions regarding use of life-sustaining procedures if the patient is able to do so or impairs or supersedes any right or responsibility that any person has to effect the withholding or withdrawal of medical care in any lawful manner. In that respect, the provisions of this act are cumulative.

Mercy killing. This act does not authorize or approve mercy killing.

Penalties. A physician who willfully fails to transfer a patient in accordance with the section on "Transfer of Patients" above is guilty of a misdemeanor punishable by a fine not to exceed $500 or imprisonment in the county jail for a term not to exceed 1 year, or both. A physician who willfully fails to record the determination of terminal condition of a patient in accordance with the section on "Recording Determination of Terminal Condition" above is guilty of a misdemeanor punishable by a fine not to exceed $500 or imprisonment in the county jail for a term not to exceed 1 year, or both. A person who purposely conceals, cancels, defaces, or obliterates the declaration of another without the declarant's consent or who falsifies or forges a revocation of the declaration of another is guilty of a misdemeanor punishable by a fine not to exceed $500 or imprisonment in the county jail for a term not to exceed 1 year, or both. A person who falsifies or forges the declaration of another or purposely conceals or withholds personal knowledge of a revocation, with the intent to cause a withholding or withdrawal of life-sustaining procedures, is guilty of a misdemeanor punishable by a fine not to exceed $500 or imprisonment in the county jail for a term not to exceed 1 year, or both.

NEVADA: WITHHOLDING OR WITHDRAWAL OF LIFE-SUSTAINING PROCEDURES (1977; amended 1985)

Execution of declaration. Any adult person may execute a declaration directing that when he is in a terminal condition and becomes comatose or is otherwise rendered incapable of communicating with his attending physician, life-sustaining procedures be withheld or withdrawn from him.

Witnesses. The declaration must be executed in the same manner in which a will is executed, in the presence of 2 subscribing witnesses, except that a witness may not be: (1) Related to the declarant by blood or marriage; (2) The attending physician; (3) An employee of the attending physician or of the hospital or other medical facility in which the declarant is a patient; (4) A person who has a claim against any portion of the estate of the declarant.

Pregnancy. If the declarant to found to be pregnant, and that fact is known to the physician, the directive to withhold or withdraw life-sustaining procedures is void during the course of pregnancy.

Entry in and removal from medical record. The executed declaration, or a copy thereof signed by the declarant and the witnesses, shall be placed in the medical record of the declarant and a notation made of its presence and the date of its execution. A notation of the circumstances and date of removal of a declaration shall be entered in the medical record if the declaration is removed for any reason.

Form of declaration. See Appendix. The declaration shall be in "substantially" this form (no specific provision is made for personalized instructions, but neither are they expressly forbidden).

Definition of life-sustaining procedure; excluded treatment. The term "life-sustaining procedure" does not include medication or procedures necessary to alleviate pain.

Revocation of declaration. A declaration may be revoked at any time by the declarant in the same way in which a will may be revoked (by a signed and dated written revocation in the presence of 2 subscribing wtinesses), or by a verbal expression of intent to revoke. A verbal revocation is effective upon communication to the attending physician by the declarant or another person communicating it on behalf of the declarant. The attending physician shall record the verbal revocation and the date on which he received it in the medical record of the declarant. No person is liable in a civil or criminal action for failure to act upon a revocation of a declaration unless the person had actual knowledge of the revocation.

Immunity when life-sustaining procedures are withheld or withdrawn. No hospital or other medical facility, physician, or person working under the direction of a physician who causes the withholding or withdrawal of life-sustaining procedures from a patient in a terminal condition who has a declaration in effect and has become comatose or has otherwise been rendered incapable of communicating with his attending physician is subject to criminal or civil liability or to a charge of unprofessional conduct or malpractice as a result of an action taken in accordance with this act.

Immunity when declaration of patient not followed. If a patient in a terminal condition has a declaration in effect and becomes comatose or is otherwise rendered incapable of communicating with his attending physician, the physician must give weight to the declaration as evidence of the patient's directions regarding the application of life-sustaining procedures, but the attending physician may also consider other factors in determining whether the circumstances warrant following the directions. No hospital or other medical facility, physician, or person working under the direction of a physician is subject to criminal or civil liability for failure to follow the directions of the patient to withhold or withdraw life-sustaining procedures.

Suicide. A person does not commit suicide by executing a declaration.

Insurance. The execution of a declaration does not restrict, inhibit, or impair the sale, procurement, or issuance of any policy of insurance, nor shall it be deemed to modify any term of an existing policy of insurance. No policy of life insurance is impaired or invalidated in whole or in part by the withholding or withdrawal of life-sustaining procedures from an insured person, regardless of any term of the policy.

Conditional execution of declaration. No person may require another person to execute a declaration as a condition for being insured for or receiving health care services.

Penalties. Any person who willfully conceals, cancels, defaces, obliterates, or damages the declaration of another without the consent of the declarant is guilty of a misdemeanor. Any person who falsifies or forges a document purporting to be the declaration of another, or who willfully conceals or withholds personal knowledge of a revocation, with the intent to cause a withholding or withdrawal of life-sustaining procedures contrary to the wishes of the declarant and thereby directly causes life-sustaining procedures to be withheld or withdrawn and death to be hastened is guilty of murder.

Termination of life. Nothing in this act permits any affirmative or deliberate act or omission which ends life other than to permit the natural process of dying.

Other right or responsibility not limited. Nothing in this act limits the right or responsibility which a person may otherwise have to withhold or withdraw life-sustaining procedures.

Effect of instrument executed before July 1, 1977. An instrument executed before July 1, 1977, which clearly expresses the intent of the declarant to direct the withholding or withdrawal of life-sustaining procedures from him when he is in a terminal condition and becomes comatose or is otherwise rendered incapable of communicating with his attending physician shall, if executed in ' a manner which attests voluntary execution and not subsequently revoked, be given the same effect as a declaration prepared and executed in accordance with this act, effective July 1, 1977.

NEW HAMPSHIRE: TERMINAL CARE DOCUMENT (1985)

Purpose and policy. The state of New Hampshire recognizes that a person has a right, founded in the autonomy and sanctity of the person, to control the decisions relating to the rendering of his own medical care. In order that the rights of persons may be respected even after they are no longer able to participate actively in decisions about themselves, and to encourage communication between patients and their physicians, the legislature hereby declares that the laws of this state shall recognize the right of a competent person to make a written declaration instructing his physician to provide, withhold, or withdraw life-sustaining procedures in the event of a terminal condition.

Who may execute a terminal care document. A person of sound mind who is 18 years of age or older may execute at any time a document commonly known as a terminal care document, directing that no life-sustaining procedures be used to prolong his life when he is in a terminal condition. The document shall only be effective if the person is permanently incapable of participating in decisions about his care.

Execution and witnesses. The terminal care document shall be executed by the person making the same in the presence of 2 or more subscribing witnesses, none of whom shall be the person's spouse, heir at law, attending physician or person acting under the direction or control of the attending physician, or any other person who has at the time of the witnessing thereof any claims against the estate of the person.

Notification. An attending physician who is requested to do so by the person executing the terminal care document shall make the document or a copy of the document a part of that person's permanent medical record.

Recommended form of declaration. See Appendix. The terminal care document may, but need not be, in form and substance substantially like the model provided. The declaration is to be notarized by a notary public or justice of the peace or other official authorized to administer oaths.

Definition of life-sustaining procedures; excluded treatments. "Life-sustaining procedures" shall not include the administration of medication, sustenance, or the performance of any medical procedure deemed necessary to provide comfort care or alleviate pain.

Physician responsibilities. An attending physician and any other physician under his direction or control, having in his possession his patient's terminal care document, or having knowledge that such a duly executed document is part of the patient's record in the institution in which he is receiving care, or who has been notified of the existence of a declaration executed under this act, shall follow as closely as possible within the bounds of responsible medical practice, the dictates of said document. In addition, the attending physician or any other physician under his control or direction who becomes aware, pursuant to this section, of such a document shall, without delay, take the necessary steps to provide for written verification of the patient's terminal condition, so that the patient may be deemed to be a qualified patient under this act. ("Qualified patient" means a patient who has executed a declaration in accordance with this act and who has been diagnosed and certified in writing to be in a terminal condition by 2 physicians who have personally examined the patient, one of whom shall be the attending physician.)

Transfer. If a physician, because of his personal beliefs or conscience, is unable to comply with the terms of the declaration, he or she shall forthwith so inform the patient or the patient's family. The qualified patient may, or the family of the qualified patient shall, then request that the case be referred to another physician. An attending physician who, because of personal beliefs or conscience, is unable to comply with the declaration pursuant to this act shall, without delay, make the necessary arrangements to effect the transfer of the qualified patient and the appropriate medical records that qualify said patient to another physician who has been chosen by the qualified patient or by the family of the qualified patient.

Revocation. A person who has validly executed a terminal care document consistent with the provisions of this act may revoke the document in the following manner: (a) By burning, tearing, or obliterating the same or causing

the same to be done by some other person at his direction and in his presence;
(b) By oral revocation in the presence of 2 or more witnesses, none of whom
shall be the person's spouse or heir at law; or (c) By written revocation, to
be signed and dated in the presence of 2 or more witnesses, none of whom shall
be the person's spouse or heir at law, expressing the intent to revoke.
Revocation shall become effective upon communication to the attending physician, who shall record in the patient's medical record the time and date when
he received notification.

Duty to deliver. Any person having in his possession a duly executed
terminal care document or a revocation thereof, if it becomes known to him that
the person executing the same is in such circumstances that the terms of the
terminal care document might become applicable, shall forthwith deliver the
same to the physician attending the person executing said document or to the
medical facility in which said person is a patient.

Immunity. An attending physician, other physician, nurse, health care
professional, or any other person acting for him or under his control, or
hospital or other medical facility within which the person may be, shall be
immune from any civil or criminal liability for any act or intentional failure
to act if said act or intentional failure to act is done in good faith and in
keeping with reasonable medical standards pursuant to the terminal care
document and in accordance with this act.

Suicide. The withholding or withdrawal of life-sustaining procedures from
a patient who has executed a document consistent with the purposes of this act
shall at no time be construed as a suicide for any legal purpose. Nothing in
this act shall be construed to constitute, condone, authorize, or approve
suicide or permit any affirmative or deliberate act or omission to end one's
own life other than to permit the natural process of dying as provided in this
act.

Conditional execution of terminal care document. No physician, health
facility, or other health provider, and no health care service plan, insurer
issuing disability insurance, self-insured employee welfare benefit plan, or
nonprofit hospital service plan shall require any person to execute a terminal
care document as a condition for being insured for or receiving health care
services; nor shall health care services be refused because a person is known
to have executed a terminal care document.

Insurance. The execution of a terminal care document pursuant to this act
shall not affect in any manner the sale, procurement, or issuance of any policy
of life insurance, nor shall it be deemed to modify the terms of an existing
policy of life insurance. No policy of life insurance shall be legally
impaired or invalidated in any manner by the withholding or withdrawal of
life-sustaining procedures from an insured qualified patient, notwithstanding
any term of the policy to the contrary.

Presumption of intent. This act shall not be construed to create a
presumption that in the absence of a terminal care document, a person wants
life-sustaining procedures to be either taken or withdrawn. Nor shall this act
be construed to supplant any existing rights and responsibilities under the law
of this state governing the conduct of physicians in consultation with patients
or their families or legal guardians in the absence of a terminal care
document.

Assisted suicide, mercy killing. Nothing in this act shall be construed
to constutute, condone, authorize, or approve assisted suicide, mercy killing,
or euthanasia, or permit any affirmative or deliberate act or omission to end

life other than to permit the natural process of dying of those in a terminal condition as provided in this act.

Pregnancy. Nothing in this act shall be construed to condone, authorize, or approve the withholding of life-sustaining procedures from or to permit any affirmative or deliberate act or omission to end the life of a pregnant woman by an attending physician when such physician has knowledge of the woman's pregnant condition.

Exception. Nothing in this act shall be construed to condone, authorize, or approve of the arbitrary withholding or withdrawing of life-sustaining procedures from mentally incompetent or developmentally disabled persons.

Document executed in hospital or nursing facility. A terminal care document shall have no force or effect if the declarant at the time of the execution of the document is a patient in a hospital or a skilled nursing facility, unless the document is signed pursuant to the requirements of RSA 551:2 and is signed in the presence of either the chief of the hospital medical staff, if witnessed in a hospital, or the medical director, if witnessed in a skilled nursing facility.

Penalty. A person who knowingly and falsely makes, alters, forges, or counterfeits, or knowingly and falsely causes to be made, altered, forged, or counterfeited, or procures, aids, or counsels the making, altering, forging, or counterfeiting, of a terminal care document or revocation with the intent to injure or defraud a person shall be guilty of a class B felony, notwithstanding any provisions in Title LXII.

Existing rights. Nothing in this act shall impair or supersede any other legal right or responsibility which any person may have to effect life-sustaining procedures in any lawful manner.

Effect of act on existing terminal care documents. Terminal care documents which have been executed prior to the effective date of this act (May 24, 1985) shall be deemed valid only if such documents substantially comply with the provisions of this act.

NEW MEXICO: RIGHT TO DIE ACT (1977)

Execution of document. An individual of sound mind and having reached the age of majority may execute a document directing that if he is ever certified under the New Mexico Right to Die Act as suffering from a terminal illness, then maintenance medical treatment shall not be utilized for the prolongation of his life. A document described in this act is not valid unless it has been executed with the same formalities as required of a valid will pursuant to the provisions of the Probate Code.

Definition. " Maintenance medical treatment" means medical treatment designed solely to sustain the life processes.

Execution of a document for the benefit of a terminally ill minor. If a minor has been certified under the Right to Die Act as suffering from a terminal illness, the following individual may execute the document on his behalf: (1) The spouse, if he or she has reached the age of majority; or (2) If there is no spouse, or if the spouse is not available at the time of the certification or is otherwise unable to act, then either the parent or guardian of the minor. An individual named in subsections (1) or (2) of this section may not execute a document: (a) If he has actual notice of contrary indications by the minor who is terminally ill; or (b) When executing as a parent or guardian, if he has actual notice of opposition by either another parent or guardian or a spouse who has attained the age of majority. A document executed for the benefit of a terminally ill minor is not valid unless it has been executed with the same formalities as required of a valid will under the Probate Code, and has been certified upon its face by a district court judge pursuant to the following: Any person executing a document pursuant to the provisions of this section shall petition the district court for the county in which the minor is domiciled, or the county in which the minor is being maintained, for certification upon the face of the document. The court shall appoint a guardian ad litem to represent the minor and may hold an evidentiary hearing before certification. All costs shall be charged to the petitioner. If the district court judge is satisfied that all requirements of the Right to Die Act have been satisfied, that the document was executed in good faith and that the certification of the terminal illness was in good faith, then he shall certify the document.

   Certification of a terminal illness. For purposes of the Right to Die Act, certification of a terminal illness may be rendered only in writing by 2 physicians, one of whom is the physician in charge of the individual who is terminally ill. A copy of any such certification shall be kept in the records of the medical facility where the patient is being maintained. If the patient is not being maintained in a medical facility, a copy shall be retained by the physician in charge in his own case records. A physician who certifies a terminal illness under this section is presumed to be acting in good faith. Unless it is alleged and proved that his action violated the standard of reasonable professional care and judgment under the circumstances, he is immune from civil or criminal liability that otherwise might be incurred.

   Revocation. An individual who has executed a document under the Right to Die Act may, at any time thereafter, revoke the document. Revocation may be accomplished by destroying the document, or by contrary indication expressed in the presence of one witness who has reached the age of majority. A minor may revoke the document in the same manner as an adult declarant; during the remainder of his terminal illness, any such revocation may constitute actual notice of his contrary indication.

   Physician's immunity from liability. After certification of a terminal illness under the Right to Die Act, a physician who relies on a document executed under this act, of which he has no actual notice of revocation or contrary indication, and who withholds maintenance medical treatment from the terminally ill individual who executed the document, is presumed to be acting in good faith. Unless it is alleged and proved that the physician's actions violated the standard of reasonable professional care and judgment under the circumstances, he is immune from civil or criminal liability that otherwise might be incurred. A physician who relies on a document executed on behalf of a terminally ill minor under the Right to Die Act and certified on its face by a district court judge pursuant to the procedure outlined in the section above, titled "Execution of a Document for the Benefit of a Terminally Ill Minor," and who withholds maintenance medical treatment from the terminally ill minor on whose behalf the document was executed, is presumed to be acting in good faith, if he has no actual notice of revocation or contrary indication. Unless it is alleged and proved that the physician's actions violated the standard of reasonable professional care and judgment under the circumstances, he is immune from civil or criminal liability that otherwise might be incurred. In the absence of actual notice to the contrary, a physician might presume that an individual who executed a document under the Right to Die Act was of sound mind when the document was executed. Any hospital or medical institution or its employees which act or refrain from acting in reasonable reliance on and in compliance with a document executed under the Right to Die Act shall be immune from civil or criminal liability that otherwise might be incurred.

Suicide. The withholding of maintenance medical treatment from any individual pursuant to the provisions of the Right to Die Act shall not, for any purpose, constitute a suicide.

Insurance. The execution of a document pursuant to the Right to Die Act shall not restrict, inhibit, or impair in any manner the sale, procurement, or issuance of any policy of life insurance, nor shall it be deemed to modify the terms of an existing policy of life insurance. No policy of life insurance shall be legally impaired or invalidated in any manner by the withholding of maintenance medical treatment under the Right to Die Act from an insured individual, notwithstanding any term of the policy to the contrary.

Conditional execution of a document. No physician, health facility, or other health care provider, and no health care service plan, insurer issuing disability insurance, self-insured employee welfare benefit plan, or nonprofit hospital service plan shall require any person to execute a document pursuant to the Right to Die Act as a condition for being insured for, or receiving, health care service.

Existing rights and responsibilities not impaired. Nothing in the Right to Die Act shall impair or supersede any existing legal right or legal responsibility which any person may have to effect the withholding or nonutilization of any maintenance medical treatment in any lawful manner. In such respect the provisions of the Right to Die Act are cumulative.

Penalties. Whoever knowingly and willfully conceals, destroys, falsifies, or forges a document with intent to create the false impression that another person has directed that no maintenance medical treatment be utilized for the prolongation of his life or the life of a minor, or whoever knowingly and willfully conceals evidence of revocation of a document executed pursuant to the Right to Die Act is guilty of a second degree felony, punishable by imprisonment in the penitentiary for a period of not less than 10 years nor more than 50 years or a fine of not more than $10,000 or both. Whoever knowingly and willfully conceals, destroys, falsifies, or forges a document with intent to create the false impression that another person has not directed that maintenance medical treatment not be utilized for the prolongation of his life is guilty of a third degree felony, punishable by imprisonment in the penitentiary for a term of not less than 2 years nor more than 10 years or a fine of not more than $5,000 or both. Whoever executes a document under the Right to Die Act for the benefit of a terminally ill minor and who either has actual notice of contrary indications by the minor who is terminally ill, or, when executing as a parent or guardian, has actual notice of opposition by either another parent or guardian or a spouse, is guilty of a second degree felony, punishable by imprisonment in the penitentiary for a period of not less than 10 years nor more than 50 years, or by a fine of not more than $10,000 or both.

Application. The Right to Die Act applies to all persons executing documents in conformity with that act on or after the effective date of the Right to Die Act (March 17, 1977).

Recommended or required form. None specified by legislature. It is suggested that you use the uniform Living Will form in Appendix B.

NORTH CAROLINA: RIGHT TO NATURAL DEATH ACT (1977; amended 1979, 1981, and 1983)

Policy statement. The General Assembly recognizes as a matter of public policy that an individual's rights include the right to a peaceful and natural death and that a patient or his representative has the fundamental right to control the decisions relating to the rendering of his own medical care, including the decision to have extraordinary means withheld or withdrawn in instances of a terminal condition. This act is to establish an optional and nonexclusive procedure by which a patient or his representative may exercise these rights.

Conditions for withholding or discontinuing extraordinary medical means. If a person has declared, in accordance with the section on "Execution of Declaration" below, a desire that his life not be prolonged by extraordinary means; and the declaration has not been revoked; and (1) It is determined by the attending physician that the declarant's present condition is terminal and incurable; and (2) There is confirmation of the declarant's terminal and incurable present condition by a physician other than the attending physician; then extraordinary means may be withheld or discontinued upon the direction and under the supervision of the attending physician.

Definition of extraordinary means. "Extraordinary means" is defined as any medical procedure or intervention which in the judgment of the attending physician would serve only to postpone artificially the moment of death by sustaining, restoring, or supplanting a vital function.

Execution of declaration. The attending physician may rely upon a signed, witnessed, dated, and proved declaration: (1) Which expresses a desire of the declarant that no extraordinary means be used to prolong his life if his condition is determined to be terminal and incurable; and (2) Which states that the declarant is aware that the declaration authorizes a physician to withhold or discontinue the extraordinary means; and (3) Which has been signed by the declarant in the presence of 2 witnesses who believe the declarant to be of sound mind.

Qualifications of witnesses. The 2 witnesses must state that they (i) are not related within the third degree to the declarant or the declarant's spouse, (ii) do not know or have a reasonable expectation that they would be entitled to any portion of the estate of the declarant upon his death under any will of the declarant or codicil thereto then existing or under the Intestate Succession Act as it then provides, (iii) are not the attending physician, or an employee of the attending physician, or an employee of a health facility in which the declarant is a patient, or an employee of a nursing home or any group care home in which the declarant resides, and (iv) do not have a claim against any portion of the estate of the declarant at the time of the declaration.

Proved declaration. The declaration must be proved before a clerk or assistant clerk of superior court, or a notary public who certifies substantially as set out in the model form.

Model form of declaration. See Appendix. This form is specifically determined to meet the requirements of this act. The addition of personalized instructions is not specifically forbidden.

Revocation. The declaration may be revoked by the declarant, in any manner by which he is able to communicate his intent to revoke, without regard to his mental or physical condition. Such revocation shall become effective only upon communication to the attending physician by the declarant or by an individual acting on behalf of the declarant.

Mercy killing. Nothing in this act shall be construed to authorize any affirmative or deliberate act or omission to end life other than to permit the natural process of dying.

Suicide. The execution and consummation of declarations made in accordance with this act shall not constitute suicide for any purpose.

Conditional execution of declaration. No person shall be required to sign a declaration in accordance with this act as a condition for becoming insured under any insurance contract or for receiving any medical treatment.

Other rights and responsibilities not impaired. Nothing in this act shall impair or supersede any legal right or legal responsibility which any person may have to effect the withholding or withdrawal of life-sustaining procedures in any lawful manner. In such respect the provisions of this act are cumulative.

Immunity. The withholding or discontinuance of extraordinary means in accordance with this act shall not be considered the cause of death for any civil or criminal purposes nor shall it be considered unprofessional conduct. Any person, institution, or facility against whom criminal or civil liability is asserted because of conduct in compliance with this act may interpose this section as a defense.

Prior certificates valid. Any certificate in the form provided by this act prior to July 1, 1979, shall continue to be valid.

Procedures for natural death in the absence of a declaration. If a person is comatose and there is no reasonable possibility that he will return to a cognitive sapient state or is mentally incapacitated, and (1) It is determined by the attending physician that the person's present condition is: terminal, incurable, and irreversible, and (2) There is confirmation of the person's present terminal, incurable, and irreversible condition, in writing by a physician other than the attending physician; and (3) A vital function of the person could be restored by extraordinary means or a vital function of the person is being sustained by extraordinary means; then, extraordinary means may be withheld or discontinued in accordance with the following. If a person's condition has been determined to meet the 3 conditions set forth and no instrument has been executed as provided in this act, the extraordinary means to prolong life may be withheld or discontinued upon the direction and under the supervision of the attending physician with the concurrence (i) of the person's spouse, or (ii) of a guardian of the person, or (iii) of a majority of the relatives of the first degree, in that order. If none of the above is available, then at the discretion of the attending physician the extraordinary means may be withheld or discontinued upon the direction and under the supervision of the attending physician. The withholding or discontinuance of such extraordinary means shall not be considered the cause of death for any civil or criminal purpose nor shall it be considered unprofessional conduct. Any person, institution, or facility against whom criminal or civil liability is asserted because of conduct in compliance with this section may interpose this section as a defense.

Death; determination by physician. The determination that a person is dead shall be made by a physician licensed to practice medicine applying ordinary and accepted standards of medical practice. Brain death, defined as irreversible cessation of total brain function, may be used as a sole basis for the determination that a person has died, particularly when brain death occurs in the presence of artificially maintained respiratory and circulatory functions. This specific recognition of brain death as a criterion of death of the person shall not preclude the use of other medically recognized criteria for determining whether and when a person has died.

OKLAHOMA: NATURAL DEATH ACT (1985)

Execution of directive. Any person 21 years of age or older may execute a directive for the withholding or withdrawal of life-sustaining procedures in the event of a terminal condition, as diagnosed and certified in writing by 2 physicians, one of whom shall be the attending physician.

Witnesses. The directive shall be signed by the declarant in the presence of 2 witnesses. Witnesses to the execution of the directive shall not be: (1) Under 21 years of age; (2) Related to the declarant by blood or marriage; (3) Financially responsible for the medical care of the declarant; (4) Entitled to any portion of the estate of the declarant pursuant to any will of the declarant, any codicil thereto, or by operation of law; (5) The attending physician; (6) An employee of the attending physician or an employee of a health care facility in which the declarant is a patient; (7) A patient in a health care facility in which the declarant is a patient; or (8) A person who, at the time of the execution of the directive, has a claim against any portion of the estate of the declarant. The signature of the declarant shall be acknowledged. Witnesses shall subscribe and swear to the directive before a notary public.

Form of directive. See Appendix. The directive shall be substantially in this form. Personalized instructions are not specifically forbidden.

Definition of life-sustaining procedure; excluded treatments. "Life-sustaining procedure" shall not include the administration of nourishment, hydration, and medication or the performance of any medical procedure deemed necessary to alleviate pain.

Revocation of directive. A directive may be revoked at any time by the declarant without regard to his mental state or competency by any of the following methods: (1) Being canceled, defaced, obliterated, burnt, torn, or otherwise destroyed by the declarant or by some person in his presence and by his direction; (2) A written revocation of the declarant expressing his intent to revoke, signed and dated by the declarant. Such revocation shall become effective only on the receipt of said revocation by the attending physician provided by the declarant or by a person acting on behalf of the declarant. The attending physician or his designee shall record in the medical record of the patient the time and date the notification of the written revocation was received and shall enter the word "VOID" on each page of the directive in the medical records of the patient; or (3) A verbal expression by the declarant of his intent to revoke the directive made in the presence of a witness 21 years of age or older who signs and dates a written confirmation that such expression of intent was made. Any verbal revocation shall become effective upon receipt of the above-mentioned writing by the attending physician. The attending physician or his designee shall record in the medical record of the patient the time, date, and place of revocation and the time, date, and place of receipt of the notification of the revocation, if different, and shall enter the word "VOID" on each page of the directive in the medical records of the patient. Except as otherwise provided for in the Oklahoma Natural Death Act, there shall be no criminal or civil liability on the part of any person for failure to act on a revocation made pursuant to this section unless that person has actual knowledge of the revocation.

Term of directive; reexecution. A directive shall be effective until it is revoked in a manner prescribed in the provisions in the section on "Revocation of Directive" above. Nothing in the Oklahoma Natural Death Act shall be construed to prevent a declarant from reexecuting a directive at any time in accordance with the formalities of this act, including reexecution subsequent to a diagnosis of a terminal condition. If the declarant becomes comatose or is rendered incapable of communicating with the attending physician, the directive shall remain in effect for the duration of the condition or until such time as the declarant revokes the directive pursuant to the provisions of the Oklahoma Natural Death Act.

Civil and criminal liability. The withholding or withdrawal of life-sustaining procedures by any physician, health facility, or other health care professionals from a qualified patient in accordance with the provisions of the Oklahoma Natural Death Act shall not constitute negligence. Further, the withholding or withdrawal of life-sustaining procedures by any physician, health facility, or other health care professionals from a qualified patient in accordance with the provisions of the Oklahoma Natural Death Act shall not constitute an offense pursuant to Sections 813 through 818 of Title 21 of the Oklahoma Statutes. Further, the withholding or withdrawal of life-sustaining procedures shall not be considered the cause of death for any civil or criminal purpose nor shall it be considered unprofessional conduct. Any person, institution, or facility against whom criminal or civil liability is asserted because of conduct in compliance with the Oklahoma Natural Death Act may interpose this section as a defense.

No physician or health care facility which, in accordance with the Oklahoma Natural Death Act, causes the withholding or withdrawal of life-sustaining procedures from a qualified patient shall be subject to civil liability unless negligent. No health care professional can use this act as a reason to withhold food, nourishment, or water to effectuate death under this act. No health care professional who participates under the direction of a physician in the withholding or withdrawal of life-sustaining procedures in accordance with the provisions of the Oklahoma Natural Death Act shall be subject to any civil liability unless negligent. No physician or health care professional acting under the direction of a physician who participates in the withholding or withdrawal of life-sustaining procedures in accordance with the Oklahoma Natural Death Act shall be guilty of any criminal act or unprofessional conduct unless negligent. No physician shall be civilly or criminally liable for failure to act pursuant to the directive of the declarant when such physician, health care facility, or health care professional had no knowledge of such directive.

Definition of qualified patient. "Qualified patient" means a patient 21 years of age or older who has been personally and independently examined by each of 2 physicians and who has been diagnosed and certified in writing by the 2 physicians to be afflicted with a terminal condition. Said written determination shall be signed and dated and filed with the patient's chart and one copy with the hospital or nursing home, where said patient is located. One physician shall be the attending physician and the other shall be chosen by the patient or the attending physician.

Verification of directive. Prior to withholding or withdrawal of life-sustaining procedures from a qualified patient pursuant to the directive, the attending physician shall verify with the patient the execution of his directive and, if the patient is mentally competent, that the directive and all steps proposed by the attending physician to be undertaken are in accord with the existing desires of the qualified patient and are communicated to the patient.

Presumption of validity. If the declarant was a qualified patient prior to executing or reexecuting the directive, the directive shall be conclusively presumed, unless revoked, to be the directions of the patient regarding the withholding or withdrawal of life-sustaining procedures.

Physician's failure to comply; transfer. No physician or health care professional acting under the direction of a physician shall be civilly or criminally liable for failing to comply with the directive of a qualified patient. An attending physician who refuses to comply with the directive of a qualified patient shall transfer the qualified patient to another physician. A failure by a physician to comply with the directive of a qualified patient may constitute unprofessional conduct if the physician refuses to make the necessary arrangements or fails to transfer the qualified patient to another physician who will comply with the directive of the qualified patient.

Patient who becomes a qualified patient after executing the directive. If the declarant becomes a qualified patient (with a terminal condition) subsequent to executing the directive and has not subsequently reexecuted the directive, the attending physician may give weight to the directive as evidence of the directions of the patient regarding the withholding or withdrawal of life-sustaining procedures and may consider other factors such as information from the affected family or the nature of the illness, injury, or disease of the patient in determining whether the totality of circumstances known to the attending physician justifies effectuating the directive. No physician and no health care professional acting under the direction of a physician shall be civilly or criminally liable for failing to effectuate the directive of the qualified patient pursuant to this subsection. (Only directives executed or reexecuted after the diagnosis and certification of a terminal condition are legally enforceable, in other words; those executed before such a terminal diagnosis will be regarded as merely advisory of the patient's wishes.)

Physician's responsibility. Without delay after the diagnosis of a terminal condition of the declarant, an attending physician who has been notified of the existence of a directive shall take the necessary steps to provide for written certification and confirmation of the terminal condition of the declarant so that the declarant may be deemed a qualified patient pursuant to the Oklahoma Natural Death Act. The failure of a physician to provide written certification of the terminal condition of the declarant pursuant to this subsection or to transfer the declarant to another physician who will so certify the condition of the declarant may constitute unprofessional conduct.

Insurance. The making of a directive pursuant to the Oklahoma Natural Death Act shall not restrict, inhibit, or impair in any manner the sale, procurement, or issuance of any policy of life insurance, nor shall it be deemed to modify the terms of an existing policy of life insurance. No policy of life insurance shall be legally impaired or invalidated in any manner by the withholding or withdrawal of life-sustaining procedures from an insured qualified patient, notwithstanding any term to the contrary in any policy in effect prior to the effective date of the Oklahoma Natural Death Act.

Conditional execution of directive. No physician, health care facility, or other health care professional and no health care service plan or insurer issuing insurance shall require any person to execute a directive as a condition for being insured for or receiving health care services. The execution or failure to execute a directive shall not be considered in any way in establishing the premiums for insurance.

Penalties. The concealment, cancellation, defacement, obliteration, or damage of the directive of another without the consent of the declarant, upon conviction, shall be a misdemeanor. The falsification or forgery of a directive of another or the willful concealment or the withholding of personal knowledge of a revocation as provided for in the Oklahoma Natural Death Act with the intent to cause a withholding or withdrawal of life-sustaining procedures contrary to the wishes of the declarant thereby, because of any such act, directly causing life-sustaining procedures to be withheld or withdrawn and death to thereby be hastened, shall be criminal homicide.

Presumption of intent. The failure of a qualified patient to execute a directive under the provisions of the Oklahoma Natural Death Act shall create no presumption as to the patient's wishes regarding life-sustaining procedures.

Construction of act. Nothing in the Oklahoma Natural Death Act shall be construed to condone, authorize, approve, or permit any affirmative or deliberate act or omission of an act to end life, other than to permit the natural process of dying as provided for in the Oklahoma Natural Death Act.

OREGON: RIGHTS WITH RESPECT TO TERMINAL ILLNESS (1977; amended 1983)

Execution of directive. An individual of sound mind and 18 years of age or older may at any time execute or reexecute a directive directing the withholding or withdrawal of life-sustaining procedures should the declarant become a qualified patient, that is, a patient diagnosed, upon examination, and certified as suffering from a terminal condition by the attending physician and one other physician.

Required form of declarative. See Appendix. The directive shall be in exactly this form (no allowance for personalized instructions is made).

Definition of life-sustaining procedure; excluded treatments. A "life-sustaining procedure" does not include the usual care provided to individuals who are in facilities defined in ORS 442.015 (12) (a) and (b), which would include routine care necessary to sustain patient comfort and the usual and typical provision of nutrition which in the medical judgment of the attending physician a patient can tolerate.

Witnesses. A directive made pursuant to this act is only valid if signed by the declarant in the presence of 2 attesting witnesses who, at the time the directive is executed, are not: (a) Related to the declarant by blood or marriage; (b) Entitled to any portion of the estate of the declarant upon the decease thereof under any will or codicil of the declarant or by operation of law at the time of the execution of the directive; (c) The attending physician or an employee of the attending physician or of a health facility in which the declarant is a patient; or (d) Persons who at the time of the execution of the directive have a claim against any portion of the estate of the declarant upon the declarant's decease.

Declarant a patient in a long-term care facility. One of the witnesses, if the declarant is a patient in a long-term care facility at the time the directive is executed, shall be an individual designated by the Department of Human Resources for the purpose of determining that the declarant is not so insulated from the voluntary decision-making role that the declarant is not capable of wilfully and voluntarily executing a directive.

Witness liable. A witness who does not attest a directive in good faith shall be liable for any damages that arise from giving effect to an invalid directive.

Revocation. A directive made pursuant to this act may be revoked at any time by the declarant without regard to mental state or competency by any of the following methods: (a) By being burned, torn, canceled, obliterated, or otherwise destroyed by the declarant or by some person in the declarant's presence and by direction of the declarant. (b) By a written revocation of the declarant expressing intent to revoke, signed and dated by the declarant. (c) By a verbal expression by the declarant of intent to revoke the directive.

Effectuation of directive. Unless revoked, a directive shall be effective from the date of execution. If the declarant has executed more than one directive, the last directive to be executed shall control. If the declarant becomes comatose or is rendered incapable of communicating with the attending physician, the directive shall remain in effect for the duration of the comatose condition or until such time as the declarant's condition renders the declarant able to communicate with the attending physician.

Presumption of validity. A directive that is valid on its face is valid as to any physician for the purposes of this act unless the physician has actual knowledge of facts that render the directive invalid or is under the direction of a court not to give effect to the directive.

Physician acting on valid directive. It shall be lawful for an attending physician or a licensed health professional under the direction of an attending physician, acting in good faith and in accordance with the requirements of this act, to withhold or withdraw life-sustaining procedures from a qualified patient who has properly executed a directive in accordance with the requirements of this act.

Immunity. A physician or licensed health professional or health facility under the direction of a physician who, acting in good faith and in accordance with the requirements of this act, causes the withholding or withdrawal of life-sustaining procedures shall not be guilty of any criminal offense, shall not be subject to civil liability, and shall not be in violation of any professional oath, affirmation, or standard of care. A physician or licensed health professional or health facility shall not be guilty of any criminal offense, shall not be subject to civil liability, and shall not be in violation of any professional oath, affirmation, or standard of care for failing to assume the duties created by or for failing to give effect to any directive or revocation made pursuant to this act unless that physician has actual knowledge of the directive or revocation.

Duties created by directive. Except as provided in this section, no physician, licensed health professional, or medical facility shall be under any duty, whether by contract, by statute, or by any other legal requirement to participate in the withholding or withdrawal of life-sustaining procedures. An attending physician shall make a directive or a copy of a directive made pursuant to this act part of the patient's medical record. An attending physician shall record in the patient's medical record the time, date, place, and manner of a revocation and the time, date, place, and manner, if different, of when he received notification of the revocation. If the revocation is written, the attending physician shall make the revocation or a copy of the revocation a part of the patient's medical record. A physician or medical facility electing for any reason not to participate in the withholding or withdrawal of life-sustaining procedures in accord with a directive made pursuant to this act shall: (a) Make a reasonable effort to locate a physician or medical facility that will give effect to a qualified patient's directive and shall have a duty to transfer the qualified patient to that physician or facility; or (b) At the request of a patient or of the patient's family, a physician or medical facility shall transfer the patient to another physician or medical facility that will reconsider circumstances which might make this act applicable to the patient.

Insurance. The making of a directive pursuant to this act shall not restrict, inhibit, or impair in any manner the sale, procurement, or issuance of any policy of insurance, nor shall it be deemed to modify the terms of an existing policy of insurance. No policy of insurance shall be legally impaired or invalidated in any manner by the withholding or withdrawal of life-sustaining procedures from an insured qualified patient.

Conditional execution of directive. No physician, health facility, health care service plan, insurer issuing disability insurance, self-insured employee welfare benefit plan, non-profit hospital service plan, or other direct or indirect health service provider shall require any person to execute a directive as a condition for being insured for, or receiving, health care services.

Withdrawal of life-sustaining procedures; conditions; physician's liability; insurance. (1) Life-sustaining procedures which would otherwise be applied to a qualified patient may be withdrawn in accordance with subsections (2) and (3) of this section if a person is comatose and there is no reasonable possibility that the person will return to a cognitive sapient state and: (a) It is determined by the attending physician that the person has a terminal condition; and (b) There is confirmation of the person's condition by a committee of physicians, not including the attending physician, appointed by the medical staff of the health facility or, if none, by the health facility in which the person is confined. (2) If a person's condition has been determined to meet the conditions set forth in subsection (1) of this section and no directive has been executed as provided in this act, life-sustaining procedures may be withdrawn upon the direction and the supervision of the attending physician at the request of the first of the following, in the following order, who can be located upon reasonable effort by the health care facility: (a) The person's spouse; (b) A guardian of the person, if any; (c) A majority of the adult children of the person who can be so located; or (d) Either parent of the person. (3) If none of the persons described in subsection (2) of this section is available, then life-sustaining procedures may be withdrawn upon the direction and under the supervision of the attending physician. (4) A physician or licensed health professional or health facility under the direction of a physician who, acting in good faith and in accordance with the requirements of this section, causes the withdrawal of life-sustaining procedures shall not be guilty of any criminal offense, shall not be subject to civil liability, and shall not be in violation of any professional oath, affirmation, or standard of care. (5) No policy of insurance shall be legally impaired or invalidated in any manner by the withdrawal of life-sustaining procedures pursuant to this section.

Withdrawal of life-sustaining procedures from comatose patient who has not executed directive. Before withdrawing life-sustaining procedures from a patient who is comatose but who has executed no directive, the attending physician shall determine that the conditions of (1) to (3) of the previous section have been met.

Mercy killing. Nothing in this act shall be construed to condone, authorize, or approve mercy killing, or to permit any affirmative or deliberate act or omission to end life other than to permit the natural process of dying as provided in this act.

Provisions of act cumulative. Nothing in this act shall impair or supersede any legal right or legal responsibility which any person may have to effect the withholding or withdrawal of life-sustaining procedures in any lawful manner. In such respect the provisions of this act are cumulative.

Suicide. The withholding or withdrawal of life-sustaining procedures from a qualified patient in accordance with the provisions of this act shall not, for any purpose, constitute a suicide.

Prohibited acts. No person shall by wilfully concealing or destroying a revocation or by wilfully falsifying or forging a directive cause the withdrawal or withholding of life-sustaining procedures. No person shall by wilfully concealing or destroying a directive or by wilfully falsifying or forging a revocation cause an individual's intent with respect to the withholding or withdrawal of life-sustaining procedures not to be given effect.

SOUTH CAROLINA: DEATH WITH DIGNITY ACT (1986)

Policy statement. Whereas, the General Assembly finds that adult persons have the fundamental right to control the decision relating to the rendering of their own medical care, including the decision to have life-sustaining procedures withheld or withdrawn in instances of a terminal condition; and whereas, in order that the rights of patients may be respected even after they are no longer able to participate actively in decisions about themselves, the General Assembly by this act provides that an adult person may make a written declaration instructing his physician to withhold or withdraw life-sustaining procedures in the event of a terminal condition.

Circumstances under which life-sustaining procedures may be withheld. If any adult declares that his dying not be prolonged and the person's present condition is confirmed by a physician other than the attending physician to be terminal, then the life-sustaining procedure may be withheld or discontinued upon the direction and under the supervision of the attending physician. All patients with life-threatening illnesses that are diagnosed as terminal shall be administered active treatment for at least 6 hours prior to the physician's acceptance of a declaration. ("Active treatment" means the standard of reasonable professional care that would be rendered by a physician to a patient in the absence of any terminal condition, including but not limited to hospitalization and medication.)

    <u>The declaration.</u> The attending physician may rely upon a signed, witnessed, and dated declaration which: (1) Expresses a desire of the declarant that no life-sustaining procedures be used to prolong dying if his condition is terminal; and (2) States that the declarant is aware that the declaration authorizes a physician to withhold or withdraw life-sustaining procedures; and (3) Has been signed by the declarant in the presence of 3 witnesses.

    <u>Qualifications of witnesses.</u> In the declaration the witnesses must state that they are not related to the declarant by blood or marriage, not directly financially responsible for the person's medical care, and would not be entitled to any portion of the estate of the declarant upon his decease under any will or as an heir by intestate succession under the laws of South Carolina of the declarant then existing or is a beneficiary of a life insurance policy of the declarant and has knowledge of such status. No more than one witness may be an employee of a health facility in which the declarant is a patient. A witness to a declaration may not be the attending physician or an employee of the attending physician or any person who has a claim against any portion of the estate of the declarant upon his decease at the time of the execution of the declaration. The declaration shall also contain an affidavit in the form of a verification by each witness that he is not disqualified by any provision of this act and such disqualification shall be set forth in the text of the affidavit.

    <u>Recommended form of declaration.</u> See Appendix. The declaration must be substantially in this form. The addition of personalized instructions is not specifically forbidden. The declaration must be signed by the declarant in the presence of the 3 witnesses and shall be attested and subscribed in the presence of the declarant and of each other by the 3 witnesses and an officer authorized to administer oaths under the laws of the state of South Carolina where acknowledgment occurs or else the declaration shall be utterly void and of no effect. (The declaration must be notarized, in other words.) See Appendix for the South Carolina affidavit form. Each will prepared in accordance with the provisions of this act shall set forth the procedure and requirements for revocation of the declaration. The law states that requirements for revocation of the declaration must be set forth in bold-face print, as shown in the model.

    <u>Definition of life-sustaining procedures; excluded treatments.</u> "Life-sustaining procedures" do not include the administration of medication nor does it affect the responsibility of the attending physician to provide treatment, nutrition, and hydration for comfort care or alleviation of pain.

    <u>Special witness requirement.</u> A declaration shall have no force or effect if the declarant is a patient in a hospital or skilled or intermediate care nursing facility at the time the directive is executed unless one of the 3 witnesses to the directive is an ombudsman as may be designated by the State Ombudsman, Office of the Governor. The ombudsman shall have the same qualifications as a witness specified above in the section on "Qualifications of Witnesses." The intent of this section is to recognize that some patients in skilled or intermediate care nursing facilities may be so insulated from a voluntary decision-making role, by virtue of the custodial nature of their care, as to require special assurance that they are capable of willfully and voluntarily executing a directive.

    <u>Pregnancy.</u> If a declarant has been diagnosed as pregnant, the declaration

shall have no force or effect during the course of the declarant's pregnancy.

Revocation. The declaration may be revoked by the declarant, without regard to his physical or mental condition: (1) By being defaced, torn, obliterated, or otherwise destroyed by the declarant or by some person in the presence of and by the direction of the declarant. (2) By a written revocation signed and dated by the declarant expressing his or her intent to revoke. The revocation shall become effective only upon communication to the attending physician by the declarant or by a person acting on behalf of the declarant. The attending physician shall record in the patient's medical record the time and date when he received notification of the written revocation. (3) By a verbal expression by the declarant of his intent to revoke the declaration. The revocation shall become effective only upon communication to the attending physician by the declarant. The attending physician shall record in the patient's medical record the time, date, and place of the revocation and the time, date, and place, if different, of when he received notification of the revocation.

Immunity. After certification of a terminal condition, a physician who relies on a declaration executed under this act, of which he has no actual notice of revocation and who withholds life-sustaining procedures from the terminally ill patient who has executed the declaration, is presumed to be acting in good faith. Unless it is alleged and proved that the physician's action violated the standard of reasonable professional care and judgment under the circumstances, he is immune from civil or criminal liability.

Failure to effectuate declaration; transfer. A failure by a physician to effectuate the declaration of a terminal patient shall constitute unprofessional conduct if the physician fails or refuses to make reasonable efforts to effect the transfer of the patient to another physician who will effectuate the declaration.

Suicide. The execution and consummation of declarations made in accordance with this act does not constitute suicide for any purpose.

Conditional execution of declaration. No person is required to sign a declaration in accordance with this act as a condition for becoming insured under any insurance contract or for receiving any medical treatment or as a condition of being admitted to a hospital or nursing home facility.

Mercy killing. Nothing in this act may be construed to authorize or approve mercy killing, or to permit any affirmative or deliberate act or omission to end life other than to permit the natural process of dying.

Presumption of intent. The absence of a declaration by an adult patient shall not give rise to any presumption as to his intent to consent to or refuse death-prolonging procedures.

Penalties. If any person knowingly provides or aids another in providing any false information of any nature in any manner relative to a declaration of a desire for a natural death under this act, including, but not limited to, the contents of the declaration or the execution or the revocation of the declaration, and life-sustaining procedures are withheld or withdrawn from the declarant and the declarant then dies as a result of that withdrawal or nontreatment, the person is guilty of murder and must be punished in accordance with the laws of this state. If any person knowingly provides or aids another in providing any false information of any nature in any manner relative to a declaration of a desire for a natural death under this act, including, but not limited to, the contents of the declaration or the execution or the revocation of the declaration, and life-sustaining procedures are withheld or withdrawn from the declarant and the declarant does not die but further expenses are incurred as a result of the withdrawal or nontreatment, in caring for the declarant, the person is responsible for the payment of those further expenses.

Coercion. Any person who coerces or fraudulently induces another person to execute a declaration under this act and the declarant dies as a result of the withdrawal of treatment or nontreatment in reliance on the declaration, that person is guilty of murder and must be punished in accordance with the laws of this state.

TENNESSEE: RIGHT TO NATURAL DEATH ACT (1985)

Legislative intent. The general assembly declares it to be the law of the state of Tennessee that every person has the fundamental and inherent right to die naturally with as much dignity as circumstances permit and to accept, refuse, withdraw from, or otherwise control decisions relating to the rendering of his or her own medical care, specifically including palliative care and the use of extraordinary procedures and treatment. The general assembly does further empower the exercise of this right by written declaration, called a "living will," as hereinafter provided.

Execution of declaration. Any competent adult person may execute a declaration directing the withholding or withdrawal of medical care to his person, to become effective on loss of competency, which declaration shall be acknowledged and signed by the declarant in the presence of 2 witnesses.

Qualifications of witnesses. The 2 witnesses shall verify in such declaration that they are not related to the declarant by blood or marriage and that they would not be entitled to any portion of the estate of the declarant upon his demise under any will or codicil thereto made by the declarant. In addition, the witnesses shall verify that neither of them is the attending physician nor an employee of the attending physician nor an employee of a health care facility in which the declarant is a patient, and neither of them has a claim against any portion of the estate of the declarant.

Notification of physician. It shall be the responsibility of the declarant or someone acting on his behalf to deliver a copy of such living will or declaration to the attending physician and/or other concerned health care provider. An attending physician who is so notified shall make the declaration, or a copy of it, part of the declarant's medical record.

Recommended form of declaration. See Appendix. The declaration may be substantially in this form, but not to the exclusion of other written and clear expressions of intent to accept, refuse, or withdraw medical care. (Personalized instructions are allowed to be added, in other words.)

Definition of medical care. "Medical care" includes any procedure or treatment rendered by a physician or health care provider designed to diagnose, assess, or treat a disease, illness, or injury. These include, but are not limited to, surgery, drugs, transfusions, mechanical ventilation, dialysis, cardiopulmonary resuscitation, artificial or forced feeding, radiation therapy, or any other medical act designed for diagnosis, assessment, or treatment or to sustain, restore, or supplant vital body function. Provided, however, that in no case shall this section be interpreted to allow the withholding of simple nourishment or fluids so as to condone death by starvation or dehydration.

(Tennessee law distinguishes between artificial or forced feeding, which may be withheld or withdrawn, and "simple nourishment," which may not.)

Definition of palliative care. "Palliative care" includes any measure taken by a physician or health care provider designed primarily to maintain the patient's comfort. These also include, but are not limited to, sedatives and pain-killing drugs, nonartificial oral feeding, suction, hydration, and hygienic care.

Definition of qualified patient. A "qualified patient" under this act means a patient who has executed a declaration in accordance with this act and who has been diagnosed and certified in writing to be afflicted with a terminal condition by 2 physicians who have personally examined the patient, one of whom shall be the attending physician.

Revocation of declaration. A declaration may be revoked at any time by the declarant, without regard to his or her mental state or competency, by any of the following methods, effectively communicated by the declarant to the attending physician or other concerned health care provider: (1) Written revocation by the declarant, dated and signed by the declarant and at least 1 witness, or notarized. (2) By oral statement or revocation made by the declarant to the attending physician. Such revocation shall be made a part of the declarant's medical record by the attending physician.

Effective date of declaration. A declaration shall be effective from the date of its execution until revoked in a manner prescribed by this act. Nothing in this act shall be construed to prevent a declarant from reexecuting a declaration at any time in accordance with the formalities of this act, including reexecution after a diagnosis of a terminal condition. If the declarant has executed more than 1 declaration, then the latest declaration known to the attending physician shall take precedence. If the declarant becomes comatose or if his condition renders him incapable of communicating with the attending physician, the declaration shall remain in effect during the comatose condition or until the declarant's condition renders him able to communicate with the attending physician.

Failure to comply; transfer; liability and penalties. Any physician or other individual health care provider who cannot in good conscience comply with the provisions of such living will, on being informed of the declaration, shall so inform the declarant, or if the declarant is not competent, his next of kin or a legal guardian, and at their option make every reasonable effort to assist in the transfer of the patient to another physician who will comply with the declaration. Any health care provider who fails to make good faith reasonable efforts to comply with the preceding procedure as prescribed by the attending physician shall be civilly liable and subject to professional disciplinary action, including revocation or suspension of license. Provided that the health care provider shall not be subject to civil liability for medical care provided during the interim period until transfer is effectuated. A physician or other health care provider who by no fault of his own has not received notice of such declaration, revocation, or other change shall not suffer civil, administrative, or criminal penalties under this act.

Willful misconduct; penalty. Any person who willfully conceals, cancels, defaces, obliterates, or damages the declaration or revocation of another without such declarant's consent, or who falsifies or forges same shall be civilly liable and subject to criminal prosecution for a misdemeanor and if a provider, subject to administrative and professional discipline.

Suicide; euthanasia; homicide. The withholding or withdrawal of medical care from a declarant in accordance with the provisions of this act shall not, for any purpose, constitute a suicide, euthanasia, or homicide.

Insurance. The making of a declaration pursuant to this act shall not affect in any manner the sale, procurement, or issuance of any policy of life insurance, nor shall it be deemed to modify the terms of an existing policy of life insurance. No policy of life insurance shall be legally impaired or invalidated in any manner by withholding or withdrawal of medical care from an insured declarant.

Conditional execution of declaration. No physician, health care facility, or other health care provider, and no health care service plan, insurer issuing disability insurance, self-insured employee welfare benefit plan, or nonprofit hospital plan, shall require any person to execute a declaration as a condition for being insured for, or receiving, health care services.

Provisions of act are cumulative. Nothing in this act shall impair or supersede any legal right or legal responsibility which any person may have to effect the withholding or withdrawal of medical care in any lawful manner. In such respect, the provisions of this act are cumulative.

Presumption of intent. This act shall create no presumption concerning the intention of an individual who has not executed a declaration to consent to the use, withholding, or withdrawal of medical care.

Signature of disabled declarant. A competent declarant, unable to sign his or her declaration, may make a signature as provided in section 1-3-105.

Provisions of act severable. If any provision of this act or the application thereof to any person or circumstances is held invalid, such invalidity shall not affect other provisions or applications of the act which can be given effect without the invalid provision or application, and to this end the provisions of this act are severable.

Immunity. No physician or health facility which, acting in accordance with the requirements of this act, causes the withholding or withdrawal of life-sustaining procedures from a patient, shall be subject to civil liability therefrom. No health care provider, acting under the direction of a physician, who participates in the withholding or withdrawal of life-sustaining procedures in accordance with the provisions of this act shall be subject to any civil liability. No physician, or health care provider acting under the direction of a physician, who participates in the withholding or withdrawal of life-sustaining procedures in accordance with the provisions of this act shall be guilty of any criminal act or of unprofessional conduct. No physician or health care provider shall be subject to civil or criminal liability or considered guilty of unprofessional conduct as a result of actions under this act which are in accord with reasonable medical standards or as a result of another physician's or health care provider's actions or failure to act in accordance with the provisions of this act.

TEXAS: NATURAL DEATH ACT (1977; amended 1979 and 1983)

Execution of directive. Any adult person may execute a directive for the withholding or withdrawal of life-sustaining procedures in the event of a terminal condition. The directive shall be signed by the declarant in the presence of 2 witnesses.

Qualifications of witnesses. A witness to the directive may not be related to the declarant by blood or marriage and may not be entitled to any portion of the estate of the declarant on his decease under any will of the declarant or codicil thereto or by operation of law. In addition, a witness to a directive shall not be the attending physician, an employee of the attending physician or a health facility in which the declarant is a patient, a patient in a health care facility in which the declarant is a patient, or any person who has a claim against any portion of the estate of the declarant upon his decease at the time of the execution of the directive. The 2 witnesses to the declarant's signature shall sign the directive.

Required form of directive. See Appendix. The directive shall be in this form.

Definition of life-sustaining procedures; excluded treatments. "Life-sustaining procedures" shall not include the administration of medication or the performance of any medical procedure deemed necessary to alleviate pain.

Revocation. A directive may be revoked at any time by the declarant, without regard to his mental state or competency, by any of the following methods: (1) By being canceled, defaced, obliterated, or burnt, torn, or otherwise destroyed by the declarant or by some person in his presence and by his direction. (2) By a written revocation of the declarant expressing his intent to revoke, signed and dated by the declarant. Such revocation shall become effective only on communication to an attending physician by the declarant or by a person acting on behalf of the declarant or by mailing said revocation to an attending physician. An attending physician or his designee shall record in the patient's medical record the time and date when he received notification of the written revocation and shall enter the word "VOID" on each page of the copy of the directive in the patient's medical record; or (3) By a verbal expression by the declarant of his intent to revoke the directive. Such revocation shall become effective only on communication to an atttending physician by the declarant or by a person acting on behalf of the declarant. An attending physician or his designee shall record in the patient's medical record the time, date, and place of the revocation and the time, date, and place, if different, of when he received notification of the revocation and shall enter the word "VOID" on each page of the copy of the directive in the patient's medical records. Except as otherwise provided in this act, there shall be no criminal or civil liability on the part of any person for failure to act on a revocation made pursuant to this section unless that person has· actual knowledge of the revocation.

Duration of directive. A directive shall be effective until it is revoked in a manner prescribed in the section on "Revocation" above. Nothing in this act shall be construed to prevent a declarant from reexecuting a directive at any time in accordance with the formalities of this act, including reexecution subsequent to a diagnosis of a terminal condition. If the declarant has executed more than one directive, such time shall be determined from the date of execution of the last directive known to the attending physician. If the declarant becomes comatose or is rendered incapable of communicating with the attending physician, the directive shall remain in effect for the duration of the comatose condition or until such time as the declarant's condition renders him or her able to communicate with the attending physician.

Civil or criminal liability. No physician or health facility which, acting in accordance with the requirements of this act, causes the withholding or withdrawal of life-sustaining procedures from a qualified patient (that is, one diagnosed and certified in writing to be afflicted with a terminal condition by 2 physicians who have personally examined the patient, one of whom shall be the attending physician), shall be subject to civil liability there-from unless negligent. No health professional, acting under the direction of a physician, who participates in the withholding or withdrawal of life-sustaining procedures in accordance with the provisions of this act shall be subject to any civil liability unless negligent. No physician, or health professional acting under the direction of a physician, who participates in the withholding or withdrawal of life-sustaining procedures in accordance with the provisions of this act shall be guilty of any criminal act or of unprofessional conduct unless negligent. No physician, health care facility, or health care professional shall be liable either civilly or criminally for failure to act pursuant to the declarant's directive where such physician, health care facility, or health care professional had no knowledge of such directive.

Verification of directive. Prior to effecting a withholding or withdrawal of life-sustaining procedures from a qualified patient pursuant to the directive, the attending physician shall determine that the directive complies with the form of the directive set out in this act, and, if the patient is mentally competent, that the directive and all steps proposed by the attending physician to be undertaken are in accord with the existing desires of the qualified patient and are communicated to the patient.

Failure to effectuate directive; transfer. If the declarant was a qualified patient prior to executing or reexecuting the directive, the directive shall be conclusively presumed, unless revoked, to be the directions of the patient regarding the withholding or withdrawal of life-sustaining procedures. No physician, and no health professional acting under the direction of a physician, shall be criminally or civilly liable for failing to effectuate the directive of the qualified patient pursuant to this section. A failure by a physician to effectuate the directive of a qualified patient pursuant to this section may constitute unprofessional conduct if the physician refuses to make the necessary arrangements or fails to take the necessary steps to effect the transfer of the qualified patient to another physician who will effectuate the directive of the qualified patient.

Directive executed prior to diagnosis of terminal illness. If the declarant becomes a qualified patient subsequent to executing the directive, and has not subsequently reexecuted the directive, the attending physician may give weight to the directive as evidence of the patient's directions regarding the withholding or withdrawal of life-sustaining procedures and may consider other factors, such as information from the affected family or the nature of the patient's illness, injury, or disease, in determining whether the totality of circumstances known to the attending physician justifies effectuating the directive. No physician, and no health professional acting under the direction of a physician, shall be criminally or civilly liable for failing to effectuate the directive of the qualified patient pursuant to this section. (Under Texas law, only a directive executed or reexecuted after the diagnosis of a terminal condition is legally enforceable; a directive executed before the diagnosis of a terminal condition shall be considered as advisory of the patient's wishes.)

Effect on offense of aiding suicide. The withholding or withdrawal of life-sustaining procedures from a qualified patient in accordance with the provisions of this act shall not, for any purpose, constitute an offense under Section 22.08, Penal Code.

Insurance. The making of a directive pursuant to this act shall not restrict, inhibit, or impair in any manner the sale, procurement, or issuance of any policy of life insurance, nor shall it be deemed to modify the terms of an existing policy of life insurance. No policy of life insurance shall be legally impaired or invalidated in any manner by the withholding or withdrawal of life-sustaining procedures from an insured qualified patient, notwithstanding any term of the policy to the contrary.

Conditional execution of directive. No physician, health facility, or other health provider, and no health care service plan, or insurer issuing insurance, may require any person to execute a directive as a condition for being insured for, or receiving, health care services nor may the execution or failure to execute a directive be considered in any way in establishing the premiums for insurance.

Tampering with directive. A person who willfully conceals, cancels, defaces, obliterates, or damages the directive of another without such declarant's consent shall be guilty of a Class A misdemeanor. A person who falsifies or forges the directive of another, or wilfully conceals or withholds personal knowledge of a revocation as provided in this act, with the intent to cause a withholding or withdrawal of life-sustaining procedures contrary to the wishes of the declarant, and thereby, because of any such act, directly causes life-sustaining procedures to be withheld or withdrawn and death to thereby be hastened, shall be subject to prosecution for criminal homicide under the provisions of the Penal Code.

Mercy killing. Nothing in this act shall be construed to condone, authorize, or approve mercy killing, or to permit any affirmative or deliberate act or omission to end life other than to permit the natural process of dying as provided in this act.

Other rights and responsibilities not impaired. Nothing in this act shall impair or supersede any legal right or legal responsibility which any person may have to effect the withholding or withdrawal of life-sustaining procedures in any lawful manner. In such respect the provisions of this act are cumulative.

UTAH: PERSONAL CHOICE AND LIVING WILL ACT (1985)

Intent statement. The legislature finds: (a) Developments in medical technology make possible many alternatives for treating medical conditions and make possible the unnatural prolongation of death; (b) Terminally ill persons should have the clear legal choice to be spared unwanted life-sustaining procedures, and be permitted to die with a maximum of dignity and a minimum of pain; and (c) Considerable uncertainty exists in the medical and legal professions as to the legality of terminating the use or application of life-sustaining procedures, even when a person in a terminal condition has evidenced a desire that the procedures be withheld or withdrawn. In recognition of the dignity and privacy which all persons are entitled to expect, and to protect the right of individuals to refuse to be touched or treated in any manner without their willing consent, the legislature declares that this state recognizes the right to make binding written directives instructing physicians and other providers of medical services to withhold or withdraw, or to provide only to the extent set forth in a directive, life-sustaining and other medical procedures.

Directive for medical services. A person 18 years of age or older may execute a directive under this act. The directive is binding upon attending physicians and all other providers of medical services. The directive shall be: (a) In writing; (b) Signed by the declarant or by another person in the declarant's presence and by the declarant's expressed direction; (c) Dated; and (d) Signed in the presence of 2 or more witnesses 18 years of age or older.

Qualifications of witnesses. Neither of the witnesses may be (a) The person who signed the directive on behalf of the declarant; (b) Related to the declarant by blood or marriage; (c) Entitled to any portion of the estate of the declarant according to the laws of intestate succession of this state or under any will or codicil of the declarant; (d) Directly financially responsible for the declarant's medical care; or (e) Any agent of any health care facility in which the declarant is a patient at the time the directive is executed.

Recommended form of directive. See Appendix. The directive shall be in substantially this form. The addition of personalized instructions is not forbidden by law.

Definition of life-sustaining procedure; excluded treatments. "Life-sustaining procedure" does not include the administration of medication or sustenance, or the performance of any medical procedure deemed necessary to provide comfort care or to alleviate pain.

Directive for medical service after injury or illness is incurred. A person 18 years of age or older may, after incurring an injury, disease, or illness, direct his care by means of a directive made under this section, which is binding upon attending physicians and other providers of medical services. A directive made under this section shall be: (a) In writing; (b) Signed by the declarant or by another person in the declarant's presence and by the declarant's expressed direction, or if the declarant does not have the ability to give current directions concerning his care and treatment, by the following persons, as proxy, in the following order of priority if no person in a prior class is available, willing, and competent to act: (i) An attorney-in-fact appointed under the section below titled "Special Power of Attorney"; (ii) Any previously appointed legal guardian of the declarant; (iii) The person's spouse if not legally separated; (iv) The parents or surviving parent; (v) The person's child 18 years of age or older, or if the person has more than one child, by a majority of the children 18 years of age or older who are reasonably available for consultation upon good faith efforts to secure participation of all those children; (vi) By the declarant's nearest reasonably available living relative 18 years of age or older if the declarant has no parent or child living; (vii) By a legal guardian appointed for the purpose of this section; (c) Dated; (d) Signed, completed, and certified by the declarant's attending physician; and (e) Signed pursuant to Subsection (b) above in the presence of 2 or more witnesses 18 years of age or older.

Qualifications of witnesses to directive for medical services after injury or illness is incurred. Same as those enumerated under the section titled "Qualifications of Witnesses" above.

Recommended form of directive for medical services after injury or illness is incurred. See Appendix. This type of directive shall be in substantially this form and shall contain a description by the attending physician of the declarant's injury, disease, or illness. It shall include specific directions for care and treatment or withholding of treatment.

Special power of attorney. A person 18 years of age or older, the "principal," may designate any other person 18 years of age or older to execute a directive under the above section titled "Directive for Medical Services after Injury or Illness is Incurred" on behalf of the principal after the principal incurs an injury, disease, or illness which renders him unable to make a directive, by executing a special power of attorney before a notary public.

Form of special power of attorney. See Appendix.

Medical services for terminal persons without a directive. (1) If a person 18 years of age or older has not executed a directive or power of attorney under this part and is unable to communicate, and the attending physician has determined that the person is in a terminal condition, life-sustaining procedures may be withheld or withdrawn under the supervision of the attending physician as provided in Subsections (2) and (3). (2) The attending physician shall consult with and obtain written concurrence in writing of: (a) a majority of 2 or 3 other physicians, that the person's condition is as described in Subsection (1), and (b) any of the following persons in the following order of priority if no person in a prior class is available, willing, and competent to act: (i) a legal guardian, if one has been previously appointed; (ii) the person's spouse, if not legally separated; (iii) the parents or surviving parent of the person; (iv) the person's child 18 years of age or older, or if the person has more than one child, by a majority of the children 18 years of age or older who are reasonably available for consultation upon good faith efforts to secure participation of all those children; (v) a legal guardian appointed for the purposes of this section; (3) If a treatment decision is made by any of the parties named in Subsection (2) other than the legal guardian, at least 2 witnesses who meet the criteria set forth in the section above titled "Qualifications of Witnesses" shall be present at the time of the decision and shall sign the document required in Subsection (2) recording the decision.

Current desires of declarant. The desires of a competent declarant, which can be determined directly or indirectly, at all times take precedence over and supersede any contrary directions contained in earlier signed directives.

Pregnancy. A directive which provides for the withholding or withdrawal of life-sustaining procedures has no force during the course of a declarant's pregnancy.

Notification to physician. It is the responsibility of the declarant or other signer of a directive to notify or provide for notification to attending physicians of the existence of a directive made under this act. Attending physicians who are notified shall make the directive or a copy of it a part of the declarant's medical records.

Revocation of directive. A directive may be revoked at any time by the declarant if the declarant has signed it personally, or by the person or persons who signed a directive on behalf of a declarant, based on changed circumstances or conditions or a change of mind, and by: (a) Being obliterated, burned, torn, or otherwise destroyed or defaced in any manner indicating an intention to effect revocation; (b) A written revocation of the directive signed and dated by the declarant or by a person signing on behalf of the declarant or acting at the direction of the declarant; (c) Oral expression of an intent to revoke the directive in the presence of a witness 18 years of age or older who signs and dates a written instrument confirming that the expression of intent was made. Any oral revocation not otherwise known to the attending physician becomes binding only upon receipt by the attending physician and other providers of medical services of a written revocation under

Subsection (b) or (c). The attending physician shall record in the declarant's medical record the time, date, and place when notice of a written revocation was received. There is no criminal or civil liability on the part of any person for failing to act upon a revocation made under this act unless that person has actual knowledge of the revocation.

Physician compliance with directive. Attending physicians and other providers of medical services have a duty to cooperate with those authorized under the circumstances set forth in this act to make written directives concerning the administering or withholding of care and treatment and shall cooperate in making good faith medical certifications as provided in this act. Attending physicians and other providers of medical services who fail to comply with this act reasonably and without undue delay, or refuse or decline to comply with directives executed under this act, shall promptly effect a transfer of the declarant to another physician or provider of medical services. Failure of an attending physician or other provider of medical services to comply with a directive executed under this act or to effect the transfer of the declarant to another physician or provider of medical services constitutes unprofessional conduct.

Presumption of validity. A directive executed under this act is presumed valid and binding and physicians and other providers of medical services shall presume, in the absence of actual notice to the contrary, that a person who executes a directive, whether or not in the presence of the physician or other provider of medical services, is of sound mind and exercised discretion in the matter. The fact a person executed a directive is not to be construed as an indication that the person was suffering from any mental incompetency.

Liability. Physicians, other providers of medical services, and their agents, who in good faith participate in the withholding or withdrawal of life-sustaining procedures or administer medical care or treatment in conformity with a directive, and persons who sign directives under this act or exercise rights on behalf of a declarant in signing a directive under this act are not subject to any criminal or civil proceeding or penalty and are not deemed to have committed an act of unprofessional conduct.

Penalties. A person who willfully conceals, cancels, defaces, obliterates, or damages a directive of another without the declarant's consent or who falsifies or forges a revocation of the directive of another is guilty of a class A misdemeanor. A person who falsifies or forges the directive of another or willfully conceals or withholds personal knowledge of the revocation of a directive with the intent to cause a withholding or withdrawal of life-sustaining procedures contrary to the wishes of a declarant, and because of this action directly causes life-sustaining procedures to be withheld or withdrawn and death to be hastened is guilty of criminal homicide.

Suicide. Neither the withholding nor the withdrawal of life-sustaining procedures in the administration of medical treatment, nor the implementation of medical treatment choices expressed in directives executed under this act constitute suicide nor the crime of assisting suicide.

Insurance. The making of a directive under this act does not affect in any manner: (a) The obligation of any life or medical insurance company regarding any policy of life or medical insurance; (b) The sale, procurement, or issuance of any policy of life or health insurance; or (c) The terms of any existing policy. A policy is not legally impaired or invalidated in any manner by the withholding or withdrawing of life-sustaining procedures or by the following of any directions in a directive executed as provided in this act, notwithstanding any terms of any policy to the contrary. Following procedures directed in a directive does not constitute legal cause for failing to promptly pay life insurance or health insurance benefits.

Conditional execution of directive. A physician or other provider of medical services, a health care service, a planned health maintenance organization, an insurer issuing disability, health, or life insurance, a self-insured employee welfare or benefit plan, a non-profit medical service corporation or mutual non-profit hospital service corporation, or any other person, firm, or entity may not require a person to execute a directive under this act as a condition for being insured for or receiving health care or life insurance contract services. However, nothing in this act may be construed to require any insurer to insure risks otherwise deemed unsuitable.

Other rights and responsibilities not impaired. Nothing in this act is intended to impair or supersede any other legal right or legal responsibility which a person may have to effect the withholding or withdrawal of life-sustaining procedures in any lawful manner.

Presumption of intent. This act creates no presumption concerning the intention of a person who has not executed a directive to consent to or refuse the use or withholding of life-sustaining or other medical procedures.

Mercy killing. Nothing in this act may be construed to condone, authorize, or approve mercy killing, euthanasia, or suicide.

Separability clause. If any provision of this act, or the application of any provision to any person or circumstance, is held invalid, the remainder of this act is given effect without the invalid provision or application.

Order of precedence of directives. When a declarant has executed a directive under the section titled "Directive for Medical Services" above and is in a terminal condition, that directive takes precedence over a non-conflicting directive executed under the section titled "Directive for Medical Services After Injury or Illness Is Incurred." A directive executed by an attorney-in-fact appointed under the section titled "Special Power of Attorney" takes precedence over all earlier signed directives.

VERMONT: TERMINAL CARE DOCUMENT (1982)

Purposes and policy. The state of Vermont recognizes that a person as a matter of right may rationally make an election as to the extent of medical treatment he will receive in the event that his physical state reaches such a point of deterioration that he is in a terminal state and there is no reasonable expectation that life can be continued with dignity and without pain. A person has a fundamental right to determine whether or not life-sustaining procedures which would cause prolongation of life beyond natural limits should be used or withdrawn.

Execution of terminal care document. A person of sound mind who is 18 years of age or older may execute at any time a document commonly known as a terminal care document, directing that no extraordinary measures be used to prolong his life when he is in a terminal state. The document shall only be effective in the event that the person is incapable of participating in decisions about his care.

Witnesses. A terminal care document shall be executed by the person making the same in the presence of 2 or more subscribing witnesses, none of whom shall be the person's spouse, heir, attending physician or person acting under the direction or control of the attending physician, or any other person who has at the time of the witnessing thereof any claims against the estate of the person.

Recommended form of terminal care document. See Appendix. The terminal care document may, but need not, be in form and substance substantially like this model.

Definition of extraordinary measures. "Extraordinary measures" means any medical procedure or intervention which utilizes mechanical or other artificial means to sustain, restore, or supplant a vital function which, in the judgment of the attending physician, when applied to the patient, would serve only to artificially postpone the moment of death and where, in the judgment of the attending physician, the patient is in a terminal state.

Action by physician. An attending physician and any other physician under his direction or control, having in his possession his patient's terminal care document, or having knowledge that such a duly executed document is part of the patient's record in the institution in which he is receiving care, shall be bound to follow as closely as possible the dictates of said document. However, if because of moral conflict with the spirit of this act, a physician finds it impossible to follow his patient's directions, he shall forthwith have a duty to so inform his patient or actively assist in selecting another physician who is willing to honor the patient's directions, or both.

Revocation. A person who has validly executed a document consistent with the provisions of this act may revoke the same orally in the presence of 2 or more witnesses, at least one of whom shall not be a spouse or a relative (as specified in 15 V.S.A. subsection 1 or 2), or by burning, tearing, or obliterating the same or by causing the same to be done by some other person at his direction and in his presence. A terminal care document may be revoked only as provided herein.

Duty to deliver. Any person having in his possession a duly executed terminal care document, if it becomes known to him that the person executing the same is in such circumstances that the terms of the terminal care document might become applicable, shall forthwith deliver the same to the physician attending the person executing said document or to the hospital in which said person is a patient.

Immunity. An attending physician, other physician, nurse, health professional or any other person acting for him or under his control, or hospital within which the person may be, shall forever be immune from any civil or criminal liability for any act or intentional failure to act if said act or intentional failure to act is done pursuant to the terminal care document.

Suicide. The withholding or withdrawal of life sustaining-procedures from a patient who has executed a document consistent with the purposes of this act shall at no time be construed as a suicide for any legal purpose.

Conditional execution of terminal care document. No physician, health facility, or other health provider, and no health care service plan, insurer issuing disability insurance, self-insured employee, welfare benefit plan, or nonprofit hospital service plan, shall require any person to execute a terminal care document as a condition for being insured for, or receiving, health care services; nor can health care or services be refused except as is hereinbefore provided because a person is known to have executed a terminal care document.

Presumptions. This act shall not be construed to create a presumption that in the absence of a terminal care document a person wants extraordinary measures to be taken.

VIRGINIA: NATURAL DEATH ACT (1983)

Policy statement. The General Assembly finds that all competent adults have the fundamental right to control the decisions relating to their own medical care, including the decision to have medical or surgical means or procedures calculated to prolong their lives provided, withheld, or withdrawn. The General Assembly further finds that the artificial prolongation of life for persons with a terminal condition may cause loss of individual dignity and secure only a precarious and burdensome existence, while providing nothing medically necessary or beneficial to the patient. In order that the dignity, privacy, and sanctity of persons with such conditions may be respected even after they are no longer able to participate actively in decisions concerning themselves, the General Assembly hereby declares that the laws of the Commonwealth of Virginia shall recognize the right of a competent adult to make an oral or written declaration instructing his physician to withhold or withdraw life-prolonging procedures or to designate another to make the treatment decision for him, in the event such person is diagnosed as suffering from a terminal condition.

Procedure for making declaration. Any competent adult may, at any time, make a written declaration directing the withholding or withdrawal of life-prolonging procedures in the event such person should have a terminal condition. A written declaration shall be signed by the declarant in the presence of 2 subscribing witnesses. An oral declaration may be made by a competent adult in the presence of a physician and 2 witnesses by any nonwritten means of communication at any time subsequent to the diagnosis of a terminal condition.

Notification of physician. It shall be the responsibility of the declarant to provide for notification to his attending physician that a declaration has been made. In the event the declarant is comatose, incompetent, or otherwise mentally or physically incapable, any other person may notify the physician of the existence of a declaration. An attending physician who is so notified shall promptly make the declaration or a copy of the declaration, if written, a part of the declarant's medical records. If the declaration is oral, the physician shall likewise promptly make the fact of such declaration a part of the patient's medical record.

Suggested form of written declaration. See Appendix. A declaration executed pursuant to this act may, but need not, be in this form, and may include other specific directions including, but not limited to, a designation of another person to make the treatment decision for the declarant should he be (i) diagnosed as suffering from a terminal condition and (ii) comatose, incompetent, or otherwise mentally or physically incapable of communication. Should any other specific directions be held to be invalid, such invalidity shall not affect the declaration.

Life-prolonging procedure; excluded treatments. "Life-prolonging procedure" does not include the administration of medication or the performance of any medical procedure deemed necessary to provide comfort care or to alleviate pain.

Revocation. A declaration may be revoked at any time by the declarant by: (1) A signed, dated writing; or (2) Physical cancellation or destruction of the declaration by the declarant or another in his presence and at his direction; or (3) An oral expression of intent to revoke. Any such revocation shall be effective when communicated to the attending physician. No civil or criminal liability shall be imposed upon any person for a failure to act upon a revocation unless that person has actual knowledge of such revocation.

Procedure in absence of declaration; no presumption. Life-prolonging procedures may be withheld or withdrawn from an adult patient with a terminal condition who (i) is comatose, incompetent, or otherwise physically or mentally incapable of communication and (ii) has not made a declaration in accordance with this act, provided there is consultation and agreement for the withholding or withdrawal of life-prolonging procedures between the attending physician and any of the following individuals, in the following order of priority if no individual in a prior class is reasonably available, willing, and competent to act: (1) The judicially appointed guardian or committee of the person of the patient if one has been appointed. This paragraph shall not be construed to require such appointment in order that a treatment decision can be made under this section; (2) The person or persons designated by the patient in writing to make the treatment decision for him should he be diagnosed as suffering from a terminal condition; or (3) The patient's spouse; or (4) An adult child of the patient or, if the patient has more than one adult child, by a majority of the children who are reasonably available for consultation; or (5) The parents of the patient; or (6) The nearest living relative of the patient. In any case where the treatment decision is made by a person specified in paragraph 3, 4, 5, or 6, there shall be at least 2 witnesses present at the time of the consultation when the treatment decision is made, and life-prolonging procedures shall not be withdrawn or withheld pursuant to paragraph 3, 4, 5, or 6 herein without the consent of at least 2 of those persons set forth in such paragraphs, provided they are reasonably available. The absence of a declaration by an adult patient shall not give rise to any presumption as to his intent to consent or to refuse life-prolonging procedures.

Transfer of patient by physician who refuses to comply with declaration or treatment decision. An attending physician who refuses to comply with the declaration of a qualified patient or the treatment decision of a qualified person or the treatment decision of a person designated to make the decision (i) by the declarant in his declaration or (ii) pursuant to the above section, "Procedure in Absence of Declaration," shall make a reasonable effort to transfer the patient to another physician. "Qualified patient" means a patient who has (i) made a declaration in accordance with this act and (ii) been diagnosed and certified in writing by the attending physician (and, in any case where the patient is comatose, incompetent, or otherwise physically or mentally incapable of communication, by one other physician who has examined the patient) to be afflicted with a terminal condition.

Immunity from liability; burden of proof; presumption. A health care facility, physician, or other person acting under the direction of a physician shall not be subject to criminal prosecution or civil liability or be deemed to have engaged in unprofessional conduct as a result of the withholding or withdrawal of life-prolonging procedures from a patient with a terminal condition in accordance with this act. A person who authorizes the withholding or withdrawal of life-prolonging procedures from a patient with a terminal condition in accordance with a qualified patient's declaration or as provided in the above section, "Procedure in Absence of Declaration," shall not be subject to criminal prosecution or civil liability for such action. The provisions of this section shall apply unless it is shown by a preponderance of the evidence that the person authorizing or effectuating the withholding or withdrawal of life-prolonging procedures did not, in good faith, comply with the provisions of this act. A declaration made in accordance with this act shall be presumed to have been made voluntarily.

Penalties. Any person who willfully conceals, cancels, defaces, obliterates, or damages the declaration of another without the declarant's consent or who falsifies or forges a revocation of the declaration of another, thereby causing life-prolonging procedures to be utilized in contravention of the previously expressed intent of the patient shall be guilty of a Class 6 felony. Any person who falsifies or forges the declaration of another, or willfully conceals or withholds personal knowledge of the revocation of a declaration, with the intent to cause a withholding or withdrawal of life-prolonging procedures, contrary to the wishes of the declarant, and thereby, because of such act, directly causes life-prolonging procedures to be withheld or withdrawn and death to be hastened, shall be guilty of a Class 2 felony.

Mercy killing. Nothing in this act shall be construed to condone, authorize, or approve mercy killing or euthanasia, or to permit any affirmative or deliberate act or omission to end life other than to permit the natural process of dying.

Suicide. The withholding or withdrawal of life-prolonging procedures from a qualified patient in accordance with the provisions of this act shall not, for any purpose, constitute a suicide.

Insurance. The making of a declaration pursuant to this act shall not affect the sale, procurement, or issuance of any policy of life insurance, nor shall it be deemed to modify the terms of an existing policy of life insurance. No policy of life insurance shall be legally impaired or invalidated by the withholding or withdrawal of life-prolonging procedures from an insured qualified patient, notwithstanding any term of the policy to the contrary.

Conditional execution of declaration. A person shall not be required to make a declaration as a condition for being insured for, or receiving, health care services.

Declarations executed prior to effective date. The declaration of any qualified patient made prior to July 1, 1983 shall be given effect as provided in this act.

Preservation of existing rights. The provisions of this act are cumulative with existing law regarding an individual's right to consent or refuse to consent to medical treatment and shall not impair any existing rights or responsibilities which a health care provider, a patient, including a minor or incompetent patient, or a patient's family may have in regard to the withholding or withdrawal of life-prolonging medical procedures under the common law or statutes of the Commonwealth.

WASHINGTON: NATURAL DEATH ACT (1979)

Legislative finding. The legislature finds that adult persons have the fundamental right to control the decisions relating to the rendering of their own medical care, including the decision to have life-sustaining procedures withheld or withdrawn in instances of a terminal condition. The legislature further finds that modern medical technology has made possible the artificial prolongation of human life beyond natural limits. The legislature further finds that, in the interest of protecting individual autonomy, such prolongation of life for persons with a terminal condition may cause loss of personal dignity, and unnecessary pain and suffering, while providing nothing medically necessary or beneficial to the patient. The legislature further finds that there exists considerable uncertainty in the medical and legal professions as to the legality of terminating the use or application of life-sustaining procedures where the patient has voluntarily and in sound mind evidenced a desire that such procedures be withheld or withdrawn. In recognition of the dignity and privacy which patients have a right to expect, the legislature hereby declares that the laws of the state of Washington shall recognize the right of an adult person to make a written directive instructing such person's physician to withhold or withdraw life-sustaining procedures in the event of a terminal illness.

Execution of directive. Any adult person may execute a directive directing the withholding or withdrawal of life-sustaining procedures in a terminal condition. The directive shall be signed by the declarer in the presence of 2 witnesses.

Qualifications of witnesses. The witnesses may not be related to the declarer by blood or marriage and may not be entitled to any portion of the estate of the declarer upon declarer's decease under any will of the declarer or codicil thereto then existing or, at the time of the directive, by operation of law then existing. In addition, a witness to a directive shall not be the attending physician, an employee of the attending physician or a health facility in which the declarer is a patient, or any person who has a claim against any portion of the estate of the declarer upon declarer's decease at the time of the execution of the directive.

Directive a part of medical record. The directive, or a copy thereof, shall be made a part of the patient's medical records retained by the attending physician, a copy of which shall be forwarded to the health facility upon the withdrawal of life-sustaining procedures.

Recommended form of directive. See Appendix. The directive shall be essentially in this form, but in addition may include other specific directions.

Definition of life-sustaining procedure; excluded treatment. "Life-sustaining procedure" shall not include the administration of medication or the performance of any medical procedure deemed necessary to alleviate pain.

Pregnancy. If a patient has been diagnosed as pregnant and that diagnosis is known to her physician, her directive to withhold or withdraw life-sustaining procedures shall have no force or effect during the course of the pregnancy.

Revocation. A directive may be revoked at any time by the declarer, without regard to declarer's mental state or competency, by any of the following methods: (a) By being canceled, defaced, obliterated, burned, torn, or otherwise destroyed by the declarer or by some person in declarer's presence and by declarer's direction. (b) By a written revocation of the declarer expressing the declarer's intent to revoke, signed, and dated by the declarer. Such revocation shall become effective only upon communication to the attending physician by the declarer or by a person acting on behalf of the declarer. The attending physician shall record in the patient's medical record the time and date when said physician received notification of the revocation. (c) By a verbal expression by the declarer of declarer's intent to revoke the directive. Such revocation shall become effective only upon communication to the attending physician by the declarer or by a person acting on behalf of the

declarer. The attending physician shall record in the patient's medical record the time, date, and place of the revocation and the time, date, and place, if different, of when said physician received notification of the revocation.
There shall be no criminal or civil liability on the part of any person for failure to act upon a revocation made pursuant to this section unless that person has actual or constructive knowledge of the revocation. If the declarer becomes comatose or is rendered incapable of communicating with the attending physician, the directive shall remain in effect for the duration of the comatose condition or until such time as the declarer's condition renders declarer able to communicate with the attending physician.

Liability. No physician or health facility which, acting in good faith in accordance with the requirements of this act, causes the withholding or withdrawal of life-sustaining procedures from a qualified patient, shall be subject to civil liability therefrom. No licensed health personnel, acting under the direction of a physician, who participates in good faith in the withholding or withdrawal of life-sustaining procedures in accordance with the provisions of this act shall be subject to any civil liability. No physician, or licensed health personnel acting under the direction of a physician, who participates in good faith in the withholding or withdrawal of life-sustaining procedures in accordance with the provisions of this act shall be guilty of any criminal act or of unprofessional conduct. ("Qualified patient" means a patient diagnosed and certified in writing to be afflicted with a terminal condition by 2 physicians who have personally examined the patient, one of whom shall be the attending physician.)

Procedures by physician; presumption of validity; transfer. Prior to effectuating a withholding or withdrawal of life-sustaining procedures from a qualified patient pursuant to the directive, the attending physician shall make a reasonable effort to determine that the directive complies with this act and, if the patient is mentally competent, that the directive and all steps proposed by the attending physician to be undertaken are currently in accord with the desires of the qualified patient. The directive shall be conclusively pre-sumed, unless revoked, to be the directions of the patient regarding the withholding or withdrawal of life-sustaining procedures. No physician, and no licensed health personnel acting in good faith under the direction of a physician, shall be criminally or civilly liable for failing to effectuate the directive of the qualified patient pursuant to this subsection. If the physician refuses to effectuate the directive, such physician shall make a good faith effort to transfer the qualified patient to another physician who will effectuate the directive of the qualified patient.

Suicide. The withholding or withdrawal of life-sustaining procedures from a qualified patient pursuant to the patient's directive in accordance with the provisions of this act shall not, for any purpose, constitute a suicide.

Insurance. The making of a directive pursuant to this act shall not restrict, inhibit, or impair in any manner the sale, procurement, or issuance of any policy of life insurance, nor shall it be deemed to modify the terms of an existing policy of life insurance. No policy of life insurance shall be legally impaired or invalidated in any manner by the withholding or withdrawal of life-sustaining procedures from an insured qualified patient notwithstanding any term of the policy to the contrary.

Conditional execution of declaration. No physician, health facility, or other health provider, and no health care service plan, insurer issuing disability insurance, self-insured employee welfare benefit plan, or nonprofit hospital service plan shall require any person to execute a directive as a condition for being insured for, or receiving, health care services.

Effects of carrying out directive on cause of death. The act of withholding or withdrawal of life-sustaining procedures when done pursuant to a directive described in this act and which causes the death of the declarer, shall not be construed to be an intervening force or to affect the chain of proximate cause between the conduct of any person that placed the declarer in a terminal condition and the death of the declarer.

Criminal conduct; penalties. Any person who wilfully conceals, cancels, defaces, obliterates, or damages the directive of another without such declarer's consent shall be guilty of a gross misdemeanor. Any person who falsifies or forges the directive of another, or wilfully conceals or withholds personal knowledge of a revocation as provided in this act with the intent to cause withholding or withdrawal of life-sustaining procedures contrary to the wishes of the declarer, and thereby, because of any such act, directly causes life-sustaining procedures to be withheld or withdrawn and death to thereby be hastened, shall be subject to prosecution for murder in the first degree as defined in RCW 9A.32.030.

Mercy killing. Nothing in this act shall be construed to condone, authorize, or approve mercy killing, or to permit any affirmative or deliberate act or omission to end life other than to permit the natural process of dying.

Severability. If any provision of this act or the application thereof to any person or circumstances is held invalid, such invalidity shall not affect other provisions or applications of the act which can be given effect without the invalid provisions or application, and to this end the provisions of this act are severable.

WEST VIRGINIA: NATURAL DEATH ACT (1984)

Execution of directive; notarization. Any person 18 years of age or older may execute a declaration directing the withholding or withdrawal of life-sustaining procedures from themselves should they be in a terminal condition. The declaration made pursuant to this act shall be: (1) In writing; (2) Signed by the person making the declaration or by another person in the declarant's presence at the declarant's express direction; (3) Dated; (4) Signed in the presence of 2 or more witnesses at least 18 years of age; and (5) Signed and attested by such witnesses whose signatures and attestations shall be notarized.

Qualifications of witnesses. A witness may not be: (1) The person who signed the declaration on behalf of and at the direction of the declarant; (2) Related to the declarant by blood or marriage; (3) Entitled to any portion of the estate of the declarant according to the laws of intestate succession of the State of West Virginia or under any will of the declarant or codicil thereto: Provided, that the validity of the declaration shall not be affected when a witness at the time of witnessing such declaration was unaware that he was a named beneficiary of the declarant's will; (4) Directly financially responsible for declarant's medical care; or (5) The attending physician, an employee of the attending physician, or an employee of the health facility in which the declarant is a patient.

Notification of physician. It shall be the responsibility of the declarant to provide for notification to his or her attending physician of the existence of the declaration. An attending physician, when presented with the declaration, shall make the declaration or a copy of the declaration a part of the declarant's medical records.

Recommended form of declaration. See Appendix. The declaration shall be substantially in this form, but in addition may include other specific directions not inconsistent with other provisions of this act. Should any of the other specific directions be held to be invalid, such invalidity shall not affect other directions of the declaration which can be given effect without the invalid direction and to this end the directions in the declaration are severable.

Definition of life-sustaining procedure; excluded treatments. "Life-sustaining procedure" does not include the administration of medication or the performance of any medical procedure deemed necessary to provide comfort, care, or to alleviate pain.

Revocation. A declaration may be revoked at any time only by the declarant or at the express direction of the declarant, without regard to the declarant's mental state by any of the following methods: (1) By being destroyed by the declarant or by some person in the declarant's presence and at his direction; (2) By a written revocation of the declaration signed and dated by the declarant or person acting at the direction of the declarant. Such revocation shall become effective only upon communication of the revocation to the attending physician by the declarant or by a person acting on behalf of the declarant. The attending physician shall record in the patient's medical record the time and date when he or she receives notification of the written revocation; or (3) By a verbal expression of the intent to revoke the declaration in the presence of a witness 18 years of age or older who signs and dates a writing confirming that such expression of intent was made. Any verbal revocation shall become effective only upon communication of the revocation to the attending physician by the declarant or by a person acting on behalf of the declarant. The attending physician shall record, in the patient's medical record, the time, date, and place of when he or she receives notification of the revocation. There is no criminal or civil liability on the part of any person for failure to act upon a revocation made pursuant to this section unless that person has actual knowledge of the revocation.

Physician's duty; chart identification. An attending physician who has been notified of the existence of a declaration executed under this act, without delay after the diagnosis of a terminal condition of the declarant, shall take the necessary steps to provide for written certification and confirmation of the declarant's terminal condition so that the declarant may be deemed to be a qualified patient under this act. ("Qualified patient" means a patient who has executed a declaration in accordance with this act and who has been diagnosed and certified in writing to be afflicted with a terminal condition by 2 physicians who have personally examined the patient, one of whom is the attending physician. Provided, that if there be more than one attending physician, all such attending physicians must certify in writing that the patient is afflicted with a terminal condition.) Once written certification and confirmation of the declarant's terminal condition is made, a person becomes a qualified patient under this act only if the attending physician verbally or in writing informs the patient of his or her terminal condition and documents such communication in the patient's medical record. If the patient is diagnosed as unable to comprehend verbal or written communications, such patient becomes a qualified patient immediately upon written certification and confirmation of his terminal condition by the attending physician. All inpatient health care facilities shall develop a system to visibly identify a qualified patient's chart which contains a declaration as set forth in this act.

Desires of qualified patient take precedence; presumption of validity. The desires of a qualified patient at all times supersede the effect of the declaration. If the qualified patient is incompetent at the time of the decision to withhold or withdraw life-sustaining procedures, a declaration executed in accordance with this act is presumed to be valid. For the purposes of this act, a physician or health facility may presume in the absence of actual notice to the contrary that an individual who executed a declaration was of sound mind when it was executed. The fact that an individual executed a declaration is not an indication of a declarant's mental incompetency.

Liability. No physician, licensed health care professional, health facility, or employee thereof who in good faith and pursuant to reasonable medical standards causes or participates in the withholding or withdrawing of life-sustaining procedures from a qualified patient pursuant to a declaration made in accordance with this act may, as a result thereof, be subject to criminal or civil liability.

Transfer. An attending physician who cannot comply with the declaration of a qualified patient pursuant to this act shall, in conjunction with the next of kin of the patient or other responsible individual, effect the transfer of the qualified patient to another physician who will honor the declaration of the qualified patient. Transfer under these circumstances does not constitute abandonment.

Penalties. Any person who willfully conceals, cancels, defaces, obliterates, or damages the declaration of another without the declarant's consent or who falsifies or forges a revocation of the declaration of another is guilty of a felony, and, upon conviction thereof, shall be fined an amount not to exceed $5,000 or be imprisoned in the penitentiary for a period not to exceed 3 years, or both fined and imprisoned. Any person who falsifies or forges the declaration of another or willfully conceals or withholds personal knowledge of the revocation of a declaration with the intent to cause a withholding or withdrawal of life-sustaining procedures, contrary to the wishes of the declarant and, thereby, because of such act, directly causes life-sustaining procedures to be withheld or withdrawn and death to be hastened is guilty of a felony, and, upon conviction thereof, shall be imprisoned in the penitentiary not less than 1 nor more than 5 years.

Suicide. The withholding or withdrawal of life-sustaining procedures from a qualified patient in accordance with the provisions of this act does not, for any purpose, constitute a suicide and does not constitute the crime of assisting a suicide.

Insurance. The making of a declaration pursuant to this act does not affect in any manner the sale, procurement, or issuance of any policy of life insurance, nor does it modify the terms of an existing policy of life insurance. No policy of life insurance may be legally impaired or invalidated in any manner by the withholding or withdrawal of life-sustaining procedures from an insured qualified patient, notwithstanding any term of the policy to the contrary.

Conditional execution of declaration. No physician, health facility, or other health care provider and no health care service plan, health maintenance organization, insurer issuing disability insurance, self-insured employee welfare benefit plan, nonprofit medical service corporation, or mutual non-profit hospital service corporation may require any person to execute a declaration as a condition for being insured for or receiving health care services.

Preservation of existing rights. Nothing in this act impairs or supersedes any legal right or legal responsibility which any person may have to effect the withholding or withdrawal of life-sustaining procedures in any lawful manner. In such respect the provisions of this act are cumulative.

Presumption of intent. This act creates no presumption concerning the intention of an individual who has not executed a declaration to consent to the use of withholding of life-sustaining procedures in the event of a terminal condition.

Construction. Nothing in this act may be construed to condone, authorize, or approve mercy killing or to permit any affirmative or deliberate act or omission to end a human life other than to permit the natural process of dying as provided in this act.

WISCONSIN: NATURAL DEATH ACT (1984)

Execution of declaration. Any person of sound mind and 18 years of age or older may at any time voluntarily execute a declaration authorizing the withholding or withdrawal of life-sustaining procedures when the person is in a terminal condition and death is imminent, which shall take effect on the date of execution. A declaration must be signed by the declarant in the presence of 2 witnesses. If the declarant is physically unable to sign a declaration, the declaration must be signed in the declarant's name by one of the witnesses or some other person at the declarant's express direction and in his or her presence; such a proxy signing shall either take place or be acknowledged by the declarant in the presence of 2 witnesses.

Qualifications of witnesses. Witnesses may not be related to the declarant by blood or marriage or entitled to any portion of the estate of the declarant upon his or her decease under any will of the declarant. The attending physician, the attending nurse, an employee of the attending physician or of the inpatient health care facility in which the declarant is a patient, or any person with a claim against any portion of the estate of the declarant upon his or her death at the time of the execution of the declaration may not be a witness to a declaration.

Notification of physician. The declarant is responsible for notifying his or her attending physician of the existence of the declaration. An attending physician who is so notified shall make the original declaration a part of the declarant's medical record.

Distribution of copies of declaration. The Department of Health and Social Services shall prepare and provide copies of the declaration for distribution in quantities to health care professionals, hospitals, nursing homes, county clerks, and local bar associations and individually to private persons. The Department of Health and Social Services may charge a reasonable fee for the cost of preparation and distribution.

Form of declaration. See Appendix. The Wisconsin Natural Death Act states that the declaration distributed by the Department of Health and Social Services shall be in this form. The law does not specifically prohibit the addition of personalized instructions.

Definition of life-sustaining procedure; excluded treatments. "Life-sustaining procedure" does not include: (a) The alleviation of pain by administering medication or by performing any medical procedure; (b) The provision of fluid maintenance and nutritional support.

Revocation. A declaration may be revoked at any time by the declarant by any of the following methods: (a) By being canceled, defaced, obliterated, burned, torn, or otherwise destroyed by the declarant or by some person who is directed by the declarant and who acts in the presence of the declarant. (b) By a written revocation of the declarant expressing the intent to revoke, signed and dated by the declarant. (c) By a verbal expression by the declarant of his or her intent to revoke the declaration. This revocation becomes effective only if the declarant or a person who is acting on behalf of the declarant notifies the attending physician of the revocation.

Recording of revocation. The attending physician shall record in the patient's medical record the time, date, and place of the revocation and the time, date, and place, if different, that he or she was notified of the revocation.

Duties and immunities. No physician, inpatient health care facility, or health care professional acting under the direction of a physician may be held criminally or civilly liable, or charged with unprofessional conduct, for any of the following: (a) Participating in the withholding or withdrawal of life-sustaining procedures under this act. (b) Failing to act upon a revocation unless the person or facility has actual knowledge of the revocation. (c) Failing to comply with a declaration, except that failure by a physician to comply with a declaration of a qualified patient constitutes unprofessional conduct if the physician refuses or fails to make a good faith attempt to transfer the qualified patient to another physician who will comply with the declaration. (A "qualified patient" means a declarant who has been diagnosed and certified in writing to be afflicted with a terminal condition by 2 physicians who have personally examined the declarant, one of whom is the attending physician.)

Effect of declaration. The desires of a qualified patient who is competent supersede the effect of the declaration at all times. If a qualified patient is incompetent at the time of the decision to withhold or withdraw life-sustaining procedures, a declaration executed under this act is presumed to be valid. The declaration of a qualified patient who is diagnosed as pregnant by the attending physician has no effect during the course of the qualified patient's pregnancy. For the purposes of this act, a physician or inpatient health care facility may presume in the absence of actual notice to the contrary that a person who executed a declaration was of sound mind at the time.

Suicide. The withholding or withdrawal of life-sustaining procedures from a qualified patient under this act does not, for any purpose, constitute suicide. Execution of a declaration under this act does not, for any purpose, constitute attempted suicide.

Insurance. Making a declaration under this act may not be used to impair in any manner the procurement of any policy of life insurance, and may not be used to modify the terms of an existing policy of life insurance. No policy of life insurance may be impaired in any manner by the withholding or withdrawal of life-sustaining procedures from an insured qualified patient.

Conditional execution of declaration. No person may be required to execute a declaration as a condition prior to being insured for, or receiving, health care services.

Other rights not impaired. This act does not impair or supersede any person's legal right or responsibility to withhold or withdraw life-sustaining procedures.

Presumption of intent. Failure to execute a declaration under this act creates no presumption that the person consents to the use or withholding of life-sustaining procedures in the event of a terminal condition.

Construction of act. Nothing in this act condones, authorizes, or permits any affirmative or deliberate act to end life other than to permit the natural process of dying.

Penalties. Any person who wilfully conceals, cancels, defaces, obliterates, or damages the declaration of another without the declarant's consent may be fined not more than $500 or imprisoned not more than 30 days or both. Any person who, with the intent to cause a withholding or withdrawal of life-sustaining procedures contrary to the wishes of the declarant, illegally falsifies or forges the declaration of another or conceals a declaration revoked under this act or any responsible person who withholds personal knowledge of a revocation and thus directly causes life-sustaining procedures to be withheld or withdrawn shall be fined not more than $10,000 or imprisoned not more than 10 years or both.

WYOMING: WYOMING ACT (1984)

Execution of declaration. Any adult may execute a declaration directing the withholding or withdrawal of life-sustaining procedures in a terminal condition. The declaration made pursuant to this act shall be in writing, dated, and signed by the person making the declaration, or by another person in the declarant's presence and by the declarant's expressed direction, and in the presence of 2 or more adult witnesses.

Qualifications of witnesses. The witnesses shall not be: (1) The person who signed the declaration on behalf of and at the direction of the person making the declaration; (2) Related to the declarant by blood or marriage; (3) Entitled to any portion of the estate of the declarant according to laws of intestate succession of this state or under any will of the declarant or codicil thereto; or (4) Directly financially responsible for the declarant's medical care.

Pregnancy. The declaration of a qualified patient diagnosed as pregnant by the attending physician shall have no effect during the course of the qualified patient's pregnancy.

Notification of physician. The declarant shall provide for notification to his or her attending physician of the existence of the declaration. An attending physician who is so notified shall make the declaration, or a copy of the declaration, a part of the declarant's medical records.

Recommended form of declaration. See Appendix. The declaration may be substantially in this form, but in addition may include other specific directions and need not include the designation of another person to make treatment decisions for the declarant.

Added personal directions severable. If any personalized directions added to the declaration are held to be invalid, the invalidity shall not affect other directions of the declaration which can be given effect without the invalid directions and to this end the directions in the declaration are severable.

Definition of life-sustaining procedures; excluded treatments. "Life-sustaining procedures" does not include the administration of medication or the performance of any medical procedure deemed necessary to provide comfort care.

Revocation. A declaration may be revoked at any time by the declarant by: (1) Being obliterated, burned, torn, or otherwise destroyed or defaced in a manner indicating intention to cancel; or (2) A written revocation of the declaration signed and dated by the declarant or person acting at the direction of the declarant; or (3) A verbal expression of the intent to revoke the declaration, in the presence of an adult witness who signs and dates a writing confirming that the expression of intent was made. Any verbal revocation is effective upon receipt by the attending physician of the above mentioned writing. The attending physician shall record in the patient's medical record the time, date, and place of when he or she received a notification of the revocation. There is no criminal or civil liability on the part of any person for failure to act upon a revocation made pursuant to this section unless that person has actual knowledge of this revocation.

Desires of qualified patient take precedence. The desires of a qualified patient shall at all times supersede the effect of the declaration. (A "qualified patient" is a declarant who has been certified to have a terminal condition by 2 physicians who have personally examined the patient, one of whom shall be the attending physician.)

Duties of physician; transfer. An attending physician who has been notified of the existence of a declaration executed under this act, without delay after the diagnosis of a terminal condition of the declarant, shall take the necessary steps to provide for written certification and confirmation of the declarant's terminal condition, so that the declarant may be deemed to be a qualified patient under this act. An attending physician who refuses to comply with the declaration of a qualified patient pursuant to this act shall attempt to effect the transfer of the qualified patient to another physician.

Presumption of validity. If the qualified patient is incompetent at the time of the decision to withhold or withdraw life-sustaining procedures, a declaration executed in accordance with this act is presumed to be valid. For the purpose of this act, a physician or medical care facility may presume in the absence of actual notice to the contrary that an individual who executed a declaration was of sound mind when it was executed. The fact of an individual's having executed a declaration shall not be considered as an indication of a declarant's mental incompetency. Age of itself is not a bar to a determination of competency.

Liability. No physician, licensed health care professional, medical care facility, or employee thereof who in good faith and pursuant to reasonable medical standards causes or participates in the withholding or withdrawal of life-sustaining procedures from a qualified patient pursuant to a declaration made in accordance with this act shall, as a result thereof, be subjected to criminal or civil liability.

Offenses; penalties. Any person who willfully conceals, cancels, defaces, obliterates, or damages the declaration of another without the declarant's consent or who falsifies or forges a revocation of the declaration of another is guilty of a misdemeanor punishable by imprisonment for 6 months in county jail, a fine of $750, or both. Any person who falsifies or forges the declaration of another, or willfully conceals or withholds personal knowledge of the revocation of a declaration, with the intent to cause a withholding or withdrawal of life-sustaining procedures contrary to the wishes of the declarant, and thereby, because of that action, directly causes life-sustaining procedures to be withheld or withdrawn and death to be hastened, is guilty of a felony punishable by imprisonment for not to exceed 20 years.

Effect of declaration. The withholding or withdrawal of life-sustaining procedures from a qualified patient in accordance with this act shall not, for any purpose, constitute a crime.

Insurance. The making of a declaration pursuant to this act shall not affect in any manner the sale, procurement, or issuance of any policy of life insurance, nor shall it be deemed to modify the terms of an existing policy of life insurance. No policy of life insurance shall be legally impaired or invalidated in any manner by the withholding or withdrawal of life-sustaining procedures from an insured qualified patient, notwithstanding any term of the policy to the contrary.

Conditional execution of declaration. No physician, medical care facility, or other health care provider and no health care service plan, health maintenance organization, insurer issuing disability insurance, self-insured employee welfare benefit plan, nonprofit medical service corporation, or mutual nonprofit hospital service corporation shall require any person to execute a declaration as a condition for being insured for, or receiving, health care services.

Other rights and responsibilities not impaired. The provisions of this act are cumulative and nothing in this act impairs or supersedes any legal right or legal responsibility which any person may have to effect the withholding or withdrawal of life-sustaining procedures in any lawful manner.

Presumption of intent. This act creates no presumption concerning the intention of an individual who has not executed a declaration to consent to the use or withholding of life-sustaining procedures in the event of a terminal condition.

Construction of act. Nothing in this act shall be construed to condone, authorize, or approve mercy killing or to permit any affirmative or deliberate act or omission to end life other than to permit the natural process of dying as provided in this act.

APPENDIX A

STATE-MANDATED LIVING WILL FORMS

STATE OF ALABAMA

DECLARATION

Declaration made this .... day of ....(Month, year). I,...............................(Name), being of sound mind, willfully and voluntarily make known my desires that my dying shall not be artificially prolonged under the circumstances set forth below, do hereby declare:

If at any time I should have an incurable injury, disease, or illness certified to be a terminal condition by two physicians who have personally examined me, one of whom shall be my attending physician, and the physicians have determined that my death will occur whether or not life-sustaining procedures are utilized and where the application of life-sustaining procedures would serve only to artificially prolong the dying process, I direct that such procedures be withheld or withdrawn, and that I be permitted to die naturally with only the administration of medication or the performance of any medical procedure deemed necessary to provide me with comfort care.

In the absence of my ability to give directions regarding the use of such life-sustaining procedures, it is my intention that this declaration shall be honored by my family and physician(s) as the final expression of my legal right to refuse medical or surgical treatment and accept the consequences from such refusal.

I understand the full import of this declaration and I am emotionally and mentally competent to make this declaration.

Signed.................................

City, County and State of Residence.......................................

Date.................................

The declarant has been personally known to me and I believe him or her to be of sound mind. I did not sign the declarant's signature above for or at the direction of the declarant. I am not related to the declarant by blood or marriage, entitled to any portion of the estate of the declarant according to the laws of intestate succession or under any will of declarant or codicil thereto, or directly financially responsible for declarant's medical care.

Witness.............................

Witness.............................

Date.................................

STATE OF ARIZONA

DECLARATION

Declaration made this ....day of ....(Month, year).
I,...............................(Name), being of sound mind, willfully and
voluntarily make known my desire that my dying not be artificially prolonged
under the circumstance set forth below and declare that:

If at any time I should have an incurable injury, disease, or illness
certified to be a terminal condition by two physicians who have personally
examined me, one of whom is my attending physician, and the physicians have
determined that my death will occur unless life-sustaining procedures are used
and if the application of life-sustaining procedures would serve only to
artificially prolong the dying process, I direct that life-sustaining procedures be withheld or withdrawn and that I be permitted to die naturally with
only the administration of medication, food, or fluids or the performance of
medical procedures deemed necessary to provide me with comfort care.

In the absence of my ability to give directions regarding the use of
life-sustaining procedures, it is my intention that this declaration be honored
by my family and attending physician as the final expression of my legal right
to refuse medical or surgical treatment and accept the consequences from such
refusal.

I understand the full import of this declaration and I have emotional and
mental capacity to make this declaration.

Signed....................................

City, County, and State of Residence...

The declarant is personally known to me and I believe him to be of sound mind.

Witness....................................

Witness....................................

STATE OF CALIFORNIA

DIRECTIVE TO PHYSICIANS

Directive made this ....day of ....(Month, year).

I, ..., being of sound mind, willfully, and voluntarily make known my desire that my life shall not be artificially prolonged under the circumstances set forth below, do hereby declare:

1. If at any time I should have an incurable injury, disease, or illness certified to be a terminal condition by two physicians, and where the application of life-sustaining procedures would serve only to artificially prolong the moment of my death and where my physician determines that my death is imminent whether or not life-sustaining procedures are utilized, I direct that such procedures be withheld or withdrawn, and that I be permitted to die naturally.

2. In the absence of my ability to give directions regarding the use of such life-sustaining procedures, it is my intention that this directive shall be honored by my family and physician(s) as the final expression of my legal right to refuse medical or surgical treatment and accept the consequences from such refusal.

3. If I have been diagnosed as pregnant and that diagnosis is known to my physician, this directive shall have no force or effect during the course of my pregnancy.

4. I have been diagnosed and notified at least 14 days ago as having a terminal condition by ...., M.D., whose address is ...., and whose telephone number is .... I understand that if I have not filled in the physician's name and address, it shall be presumed that I did not have a terminal condition when I made out this directive.

5. This directive shall have no force or effect five years from the date filled in above.

6. I understand the full import of this directive and I am emotionally and mentally competent to make this directive.

Signed...

City, County and State of Residence..................................

The declarant has been personally known to me and I believe him or her to be of sound mind.

Witness..

Witness..

STATE OF COLORADO

DECLARATION AS TO MEDICAL OR SURGICAL TREATMENT

I,.......................................(Name), being of sound mind and at least eighteen years of age, direct that my life shall not be artificially prolonged under the circumstances set forth below and hereby declare that:

1. If at any time my attending physician and one other physician certify in writing that:

a. I have an injury, disease, or illness which is not curable or reversible and which, in their judgment, is a terminal condition; and

b. For a period of forty-eight consecutive hours or more, I have been unconscious, comatose, or otherwise incompetent so as to be unable to make or communicate responsible decisions concerning my person; then

I direct that life-sustaining procedures shall be withdrawn and withheld; it being understood that life-sustaining procedures shall not include any medical procedure or intervention for nourishment or considered necessary by the attending physician to provide comfort or alleviate pain.

2. I execute this declaration, as my free and voluntary act this........ day of........................(Month, year).

By.......................................
Declarant

The foregoing instrument was signed and declared by ....
to be his declaration, in the presence of us, who, in his presence, in the presence of each other, and at his request, have signed our names below as witnesses, and we declare that, at the time of the execution of this instrument, the declarant, according to our best knowledge and belief, was of sound mind and under no constraint or undue influence.

Dated at...................., Colorado, this......day of..........,19...

....
Name and Address

....
Name and Address

STATE OF COLORADO)
) ss.
County of_____)

SUBSCRIBED and sworn to before me by ....,
the declarant, and...and
................................., witnesses, as the voluntary act and deed
of the declarant, this.......day of ...., 19........

My commission expires:

Notary Public

STATE OF CONNECTICUT

LIVING WILL DOCUMENT

    If the time comes when I am incapacitated to the point when I can no longer actively take part in decisions for my own life, and am unable to direct my physician as to my own medical care, I wish this statement to stand as a testament of my wishes. I.......................................(NAME) request that I be allowed to die and not be kept alive through life support systems if my condition is deemed terminal. I do not intend any direct taking of my life, but only that my dying not be unreasonably prolonged. This request is made, after careful reflection, while I am of sound mind.

                               ....(Signature)

                               ....(Date)

...................................(Witness)

...................................(Witness)

DISTRICT OF COLUMBIA

DECLARATION

Declaration made this ......day of ....(Month, year).

I, ...(NAME), being of sound mind, willfully and voluntarily make known my desires that my dying shall not be artificially prolonged under the circumstances set forth below, do declare:

If at any time I should have an incurable injury, disease, or illness certified to be a terminal condition by 2 physicians who have personally examined me, one of whom shall be my attending physician, and the physicians have determined that my death will occur whether or not life-sustaining procedures are utilized and where the application of life-sustaining procedures would serve only to artificially prolong the dying process, I direct that such procedures be withheld or withdrawn, and that I be permitted to die naturally with only the administration of medication or the performance of any medical procedure deemed necessary to provide me with comfort care or to alleviate pain.

In the absence of my ability to give directions regarding the use of such life-sustaining procedures, it is my intention that this declaration shall be honored by my family and physician(s) as the final expression of my legal right to refuse medical or surgical treatment and accept the consequences from such refusal.

I understand the full import of this declaration and I am emotionally and mentally competent to make this declaration.

Signed.................................

Address...............................

I believe the declarant to be of sound mind. I did not sign the declarant's signature above for or at the direction of the declarant. I am at least 18 years of age and am not related to the declarant by blood or marriage, entitled to any portion of the estate of the declarant according to the laws of intestate succession of the District of Columbia or under any will of the declarant or codicil thereto, or directly financially responsible for declarant's medical care. I am not the declarant's attending physician, an employee of the attending physician, or an employee of the health facility in which the declarant is a patient.

Witness..............................

Witness..............................

STATE OF FLORIDA

DECLARATION

Declaration made this........day of.....................(Month, year).

I, ...(NAME), willfully and voluntarily make
known my desire that my dying not be artificially prolonged under the circumstances set forth below, and I do hereby declare:

If at any time I should have a terminal condition and my attending
physician has determined that there can be no recovery from such condition and
that my death is imminent, I direct that life-prolonging procedures be withheld
or withdrawn when the application of such procedures would serve only to
prolong artificially the process of dying, and that I be permitted to die
naturally with only the administration of medication or the performance of any
medical procedure deemed necessary to provide me with comfort care or to
alleviate pain.

In the absence of my ability to give directions regarding the use of such
life-prolonging procedures, it is my intention that this declaration be honored
by my family and physician as the final expression of my legal right to refuse
medical or surgical treatment and to accept the consequences for such refusal.

If I have been diagnosed as pregnant and that diagnosis is known to my
physician, this declaration shall have no force or effect during the course of
my pregnancy.

I understand the full import of this declaration, and I am emotionally and
mentally competent to make this declaration.

Signed...............................

The declarant is known to me, and I believe him or her to be of sound
mind.

Witness..............................

Witness..............................

STATE OF GEORGIA

"LIVING WILL

Living will made this.......day of........................(Month, year).

I,................................., being of sound mind, willfully and voluntarily make known my desire that my life shall not be prolonged under the circumstances set forth below and do declare:

1. If at any time I should have a terminal condition as defined in and established in accordance with the procedures set forth in paragraph (10) of Code Section 31-32-2 of the Official Code of Georgia Annotated, I direct that the application of life-sustaining procedures to my body be withheld or withdrawn and that I be permitted to die;

2. In the absence of my ability to give directions regarding the use of such life-sustaining procedures, it is my intention that this living will shall be honored by my family and physician(s) as the final expression of my legal right to refuse medical or surgical treatment and accept the consequences from such refusal;

3. This will shall have no force or effect seven years from the date I signed this document as stated above; however, I understand that, if at the end of said seven years I am incapable of communicating with the attending physician, this will shall remain in effect until such time as I am able to communicate with the physician;

4. I understand that I may revoke this living will at any time;

5. I understand the full import of this living will, and I am at least 18 years of age and am emotionally and mentally competent to make this living will; and

6. If I have been diagnosed as pregnant, this living will shall have no force and effect during the course of my pregnancy.

                              Signed...............................

....................(City),........................(County), and

.......................(State of Residence).

I hereby witness this living will and attest that:

(1) The declarant is personally known to me and I believe the declarant to be at least 18 years of age and of sound mind;

(2) I am at least 18 years of age;

(3)   To the best of my knowledge, at the time of the execution of this living will, I:

(A)   Am not related to the declarant by blood or marriage;

(B)   Would not be entitled to any portion of the declarant's estate by any will or by operation of law under the rules of descent and distribution of this state;

(C)   Am not the attending physician of declarant or an employee of the attending physician or an employee of the hospital or skilled nursing facility in which declarant is a patient;

(D)   Am not directly financially responsible for the declarant's medical care; and

(E)   Have no present claim against any portion of the estate of the declarant;

(4) Declarant has signed this document in my presence as above-instructed, on the date above first shown.

                    Witness...................................

                    Address...................................

                    Witness...................................

                    Address...................................

Additional witness required when living will is signed in a hospital or skilled nursing facility.

I hereby witness this living will and attest that I believe the declarant to be of sound mind and to have made this living will willingly and voluntarily.

            Witness:......................................
            Medical director of skilled nursing facility
                 or chief of the hospital medical staff"

STATE OF IDAHO

DIRECTIVE TO PHYSICIAN

Directive made this........day of.........................(Month, year).

I,................................., being of sound mind, willfully and voluntarily make known my desire that my life shall not be artificially prolonged under the circumstances below:

1. In the absence of my ability to give directions regarding the use of artificial life-sustaining procedures as a result of the disease process of my terminal condition, it is my intention that such artificial life-sustaining procedures should not be used when they would serve only to artificially prolong the moment of my death and where my attending physician determines that my death is imminent whether or not the artificial life-sustaining procedures are utilized.

2. I have been diagnosed and notified that I have a terminal condition known as.............................by................................., M.D., whose address is.........................and whose telephone number is.........

3. This directive shall have no force or effect after five years from the date filled in above.

4. I understand the full impact of this directive and I am emotionally and mentally competent to make this directive.

....
(Name)

....
(City, County and State)

....
Witness

....
Witness

STATE OF IDAHO)
) ss.
County of Ada
    We, ..., ..., and ...., the Qualified Patient and the witnesses respectively, whose names are signed to the attached and foregoing instrument, being first duly sworn, do hereby declare to the undersigned authority that the Qualified Patient signed and executed the Directive and that he signed willingly and he executed it as his free and voluntary act for the purposes therein expressed; and that each of the witnesses, in the presence and hearing of the

Qualified Patient signed the Directive as witness and that to the best of his knowledge the Qualified Patient was at the time 18 or more years of age, of sound mind and under no constraint or undue influence. We the undersigned witnesses further declare that we are not related to the Qualified Patient by blood or marriage; that we are not entitled to any portion of the estate of the Qualified Patient upon his decease under any will or codicil thereto presently existing or by operation of law then existing; that we are not the attending physician, an employee of the attending physician or a health facility in which the Qualified Patient is a patient, and that we are not a person who has a claim against any portion of the estate of the Qualified Patient upon his decease at the present time.

....
Qualified Patient

....
Witness

....
Witness

    SUBSCRIBED, sworn to and acknowledged before me by........................
................., the Qualified Patient, and subscribed and sworn to before me by.. and....................................,
witnesses, this.......day of........................., 19........

....
Notary Public for the State of
Idaho
Residing at Boise, Idaho

(SEAL)

STATE OF ILLINOIS

DECLARATION

Declaration made this........day of.......................(Month, year).
I, ...(NAME), being of sound mind, willfully and
voluntarily make known my desires that my moment of death shall not be artificially postponed under the circumstances set forth below, do hereby declare:

If at any time I should have an incurable injury, disease, or illness
judged to be a terminal condition by my attending physician who has personally
examined me, and has determined that my death is imminent except for life-sustaining procedures, I direct that such procedures be withheld or withdrawn, and
that I be permitted to die naturally with only the administration of medication, sustenance, or the performance of any medical procedure deemed necessary
to provide me with comfort care.

In the absence of my ability to give directions regarding the use of such
life-sustaining procedures, it is my intention that this declaration shall be
honored by my family and physician as the final expression of my legal right to
refuse medical or surgical treatment and accept the consequences from such
refusal.

I understand the full import of this declaration and I am emotionally and
mentally competent to make this declaration.

Signed................................

City, County and State of Residence...

The declarant has been personally known to me and I believe him or her to be of
sound mind. I did not sign the declarant's signature above for or at the
direction of the declarant. I am not related to the declarant by blood or
marriage, entitled to any portion of the estate of the declarant according to
the laws of intestate succession or under any will of declarant or codicil
thereto, or directly financially responsible for declarant's medical care.

Witness................................

Witness................................

STATE OF INDIANA

LIVING WILL DECLARATION

Declaration made this........day of.......................(Month, year).
I, ...(NAME), being at least eighteen (18) years
old and of sound mind, willfully and voluntarily make known my desires that my
dying shall not be artificially prolonged under the circumstances set forth
below, and I declare:

   If at any time I have an incurable injury, disease, or illness certified
in writing to be a terminal condition by my attending physician, and my
attending physician has determined that my death will occur within a short
period of time, and the use of life-prolonging procedures would serve only to
artificially prolong the dying process, I direct that such procedures be
withheld or withdrawn, and that I be permitted to die naturally with only the
provision of appropriate nutrition and hydration and the administration of
medication and the performance of any medical procedure necessary to provide me
with comfort care or to alleviate pain.

   In the absence of my ability to give directions regarding the use of
life-prolonging procedures, it is my intention that this declaration be honored
by my family and physician as the final expression of my legal right to refuse
medical or surgical treatment and accept the consequences of the refusal.

   I understand the full import of this declaration.

                              Signed..................................

City, County, and State of Residence...

   The declarant has been personally known to me, and I believe (him/her) to
be of sound mind. I did not sign the declarant's signature above for or at the
direction of the declarant. I am not a parent, spouse, or child of the
declarant. I am not entitled to any part of the declarant's estate or directly
financially responsible for the declarant's medical care. I am competent and
at least eighteen (18) years old.

      Witness........................... Date...........................

      Witness........................... Date...........................

****
INDIANA LIFE-PROLONGING PROCEDURES DECLARATION

Declaration made this........day of.......................(Month, year).
I, ...(NAME), being at least eighteen (18) years
old and of sound mind, willfully and voluntarily make known my desire that if
at any time I have an incurable injury, disease, or illness determined to be a

terminal condition I request the use of life-prolonging procedures that would extend my life.   This includes appropriate nutrition and hydration, the administration of medication, and the performance of all other medical procedures necessary to extend my life, to provide comfort care, or to alleviate pain.

In the absence of my ability to give directions regarding the use of life-prolonging procedures, it is my intention that this declaration be honored by my family and physician as the final expression of my legal right to request medical or surgical treatment and accept the consequences of the request.

I understand the full import of this declaration.

Signed...................................

City, County, and State of Residence...

The declarant has been personally known to me, and I believe (him/her) to be of sound mind. I am competent and at least eighteen (18) years old.

Witness.......................... Date...........................

Witness.......................... Date...........................

STATE OF IOWA

DECLARATION

    If I should have an incurable or irreversible condition that will cause my death within a relatively short time, it is my desire that my life not be prolonged by administration of life-sustaining procedures. If my condition is terminal and I am unable to participate in decisions regarding my medical treatment, I direct my attending physician to withhold or withdraw procedures that merely prolong the dying process and are not necessary to my comfort or freedom from pain.

            Signed this........day of...............(Month, year).

            Signature..

City, County, and State of Residence..

    The declarant is known to me and voluntarily signed this document in my presence.

            Witness..

            Address..

            Witness..

            Address..

STATE OF KANSAS

DECLARATION

Declaration made this........day of......................(Month, year).
I, ...(NAME), being of sound mind, willfully and
voluntarily make known my desire that my dying shall not be artificially
prolonged under the circumstances set forth below, do hereby declare:

If at any time I should have an incurable injury, disease, or illness
certified to be a terminal condition by two physicians who have personally
examined me, one of whom shall be my attending physician, and the physicians
have determined that my death will occur whether or not life-sustaining
procedures are utilized and where the application of life-sustaining procedures
would serve only to artificially prolong the dying process, I direct that such
procedures be withheld or withdrawn, and that I be permitted to die naturally
with only the administration of medication or the performance of any medical
procedure deemed necessary to provide me with comfort care.

In the absence of my ability to give directions regarding the use of such
life-sustaining procedures, it is my intention that this declaration shall be
honored by my family and physician(s) as the final expression of my legal right
to refuse medical or surgical treatment and accept the consequences from such
refusal.

I understand the full import of this declaration and I am emotionally and
mentally competent to make this declaration.

Signed...

City, County, and State of Residence...

The declarant has been personally known to me and I believe him or her to
be of sound mind. I did not sign the declarant's signature above for or at the
direction of the declarant. I am not related to the declarant by blood or
marriage, entitled to any portion of the estate of the declarant according to
the laws of intestate succession or under any will of declarant or codicil
thereto, or directly financially responsible for declarant's medical care.

Witness...

Witness...

STATE OF LOUISIANA

DECLARATION

Declaration made this........day of......................(Month, year).

I, ...(NAME), being of sound mind, willfully and voluntarily make known my desire that my dying shall not be artificially prolonged under the circumstances set forth below and do hereby declare:

If at any time I should have an incurable injury, disease, or illness certified to be a terminal and irreversible condition by two physicians who have personally examined me, one of whom shall be my attending physician, and the physicians have determined that my death will occur whether or not life-sustaining procedures are utilized and where the application of life-sustaining procedures would serve only to prolong artificially the dying process, I direct that such procedures be withheld or withdrawn and that I be permitted to die naturally with only the administration of medication or the performance of any medical procedure deemed necessary to provide me with comfort care.

In the absence of my ability to give directions regarding the use of such life-sustaining procedures, it is my intention that this declaration shall be honored by my family and physician(s) as the final expression of my legal right to refuse medical or surgical treatment and accept the consequences from such refusal.

I understand the full import of this declaration and I am emotionally and mentally competent to make this declaration.

Signed...

City, Parish, and State of Residence...

The declarant has been personally known to me and I believe him or her to be of sound mind.

Witness......................................

Witness......................................

STATE OF MAINE

DECLARATION

If I should have an incurable or irreversible condition that will cause my death within a short time, and if I am unable to participate in decisions regarding my medical treatment, I direct my attending physician to withhold or withdraw procedures that merely prolong the dying process and are not necessary to my comfort or freedom from pain.

Signed this........day of.....................................(Month, year).
        date

                Signature...

City, County, and
State of Residence...
               city   county   state

The declarant is known to me and voluntarily signed this document in my presence.

        Witness...

        Address...

               ....

        Witness...

        Address...

               ....

STATE OF MARYLAND

"DECLARATION

If at any time I should have an incurable injury, disease, or illness certified to be a terminal condition by two (2) physicians who have personally examined me, one (1) of whom shall be my attending physician, and the physicians have determined that my death is imminent and will occur whether or not life-sustaining procedures are utilized and where the application of such procedures would serve only to artificially prolong the dying process, I direct that such procedures be withheld or withdrawn, and that I be permitted to die naturally with only the administration of medication, the administration of food and water, and the performance of any medical procedure that is necessary to provide comfort care or alleviate pain. In the absence of my ability to give directions regarding the use of such life-sustaining procedures, it is my intention that this declaration shall be honored by my family and physician(s) as the final expression of my right to control my medical care and treatment.

Declaration made this........day of........................(Month, year). I, ...(NAME), being of sound mind, willfully and voluntarily direct that my dying shall not be artificially prolonged under the circumstances set forth in this declaration:

I am legally competent to make this declaration, and I understand its full import.

Signed..

Address...

....

Under penalty of perjury, we state that this declaration was signed by .... in the presence of the undersigned who, at .... request, in .... presence, and in the presence of each other, have hereunto signed our names and witnessed this........day of.............. 19....., and declare: The declarant is personally known to me, and I believe the declarant to be of sound mind. I did not sign the declarant's signature to this declaration. Based upon information and belief, I am not related to the declarant by blood or marriage, a creditor of the declarant, entitled to any portion of the estate of the declarant under any existing testamentary instrument of the declarant, financially or otherwise responsible for the declarant's medical care, or an employee of any such person or institution.

.... Address....................................

....

.... Address....................................

...."

STATE OF MISSISSIPPI

DECLARATION OF INTENT

DECLARATION made on..............(date) by...................(person's name) of .... (address), ...(Social Security Number).

I, ...(NAME), being of sound mind, declare that if at any time I should suffer a terminal physical condition which causes me severe distress or unconsciousness, and my physician, with the concurrence of two (2) other physicians, believes that there is no expectation of my regaining consciousness or a state of health that is meaningful to me and but for the use of life-sustaining mechanisms my death would be imminent, I desire that the mechanisms be withdrawn so that I may die naturally. However, if I have been diagnosed as pregnant and that diagnosis is known to my physician, this declaration shall have no force or effect during the course of my pregnancy. I further declare that this declaration shall be honored by my family and my physician as the final expression of my desires concerning the manner in which I die.

SIGNED...

I hereby witness this declaration and attest that:
(1) I personally know the Declarant and believe the Declarant to be of sound mind.
(2) To the best of my knowledge, at the time of the execution of this declaration, I:
(a) Am not related to the Declarant by blood or marriage,
(b) Do not have any claim on the estate of the Declarant,
(c) Am not entitled to any portion of the Declarant's estate by any will or by operation of law, and
(d) Am not a physician attending the Declarant or a person employed by a physician attending the Declarant.

WITNESS...

ADDRESS...

SOCIAL SECURITY NUMBER..................................

WITNESS...

ADDRESS...

SOCIAL SECURITY NUMBER..................................

STATE OF MISSISSIPPI

REVOCATION OF DECLARATION

On................(date), I, ..., (person's name),
of .... (address), ... (Social Security Number),
being of sound mind, revoke the declaration made on.....................(date
declaration made) regarding the manner in which I die.

SIGNED......................................

I hereby witness this revocation and attest that:

(1) I personally know the maker of this revocation and believe the maker
of this revocation to be of sound mind.

(2) To the best of my knowledge, at the time of the execution of this
revocation, I:

(a) Am not related to the maker of this revocation by blood or marriage,

(b) Do not have any claim on the estate of the maker of this revocation,

(c) Am not entitled to any portion of the estate of the maker of this
revocation by any will or by operation of law, and

(d) Am not a physician attending the maker of the revocation or a person
employed by a physician attending the maker of this revocation.

WITNESS......................................

ADDRESS......................................

SOCIAL SECURITY NUMBER......................................

WITNESS......................................

ADDRESS......................................

SOCIAL SECURITY NUMBER......................................

STATE OF MISSOURI

DECLARATION

I have the primary right to make my own decisions concerning treatment that might unduly prolong the dying process. By this declaration I express to my physician, family, and friends my intent. If I should have a terminal condition it is my desire that my dying not be prolonged by administration of death-prolonging procedures. If my condition is terminal and I am unable to participate in decisions regarding my medical treatment, I direct my attending physician to withhold or withdraw medical procedures that merely prolong the dying process and are not necessary to my comfort or to alleviate pain. It is not my intent to authorize affirmative or deliberate acts or omissions to shorten my life rather only to permit the natural process of dying.

Signed this........day of...............................(Month, year)

Signature...

City, County, and State of Residence..

The declarant is known to me, is eighteen years of age or older, of sound mind, and voluntarily signed this document in my presence.

Witness...

Address...

Witness...

Address...

REVOCATION PROVISION

I hereby revoke the above declaration,   Signed...................
                                                        (Signature of Declarant)

Date..

STATE OF MONTANA

DECLARATION

If I should have an incurable or irreversible condition that will cause my death within a relatively short time, it is my desire that my life not be prolonged by administration of life-sustaining procedures. If my condition is terminal and I am unable to participate in decisions regarding my medical treatment, I direct my attending physician to withhold or withdraw procedures that merely prolong the dying process and are not necessary to my comfort or freedom from pain. It is my intention that this declaration shall be valid until revoked by me.

Signed this........day of....................................(Month, year)

Signature...

City, County, and State of Residence......................................

The declarant is known to me and voluntarily signed this document in my presence.

Witness...

Address...

Witness...

Address...

STATE OF NEVADA

DIRECTIVE TO PHYSICIANS

Date..

I, ...(NAME), being of sound mind, intentionally and voluntarily declare:

1. If at any time I am in a terminal condition and become comatose or am otherwise rendered incapable of communicating with my attending physician, and my death is imminent because of an incurable disease, illness, or injury, I direct that life sustaining procedures be withheld or withdrawn, and that I be permitted to die naturally.

2. It is my intention that this directive be honored by my family and attending physician as the final expression of my legal right to refuse medical or surgical treatment and to accept the consequences of my refusal.

3. If I have been found to be pregnant, and that fact is known to my physician, this directive is void during the course of my pregnancy. I understand the full import of this directive, and I am emotionally and mentally competent to execute it.

Signed..

City, County, and State of Residence...

The declarant has been personally known to me and I believe ....
.... to be of sound mind.

Witness......................................

Witness......................................

(Section 3 of the declaration form should be omitted for male declarants.)

STATE OF NEW HAMPSHIRE

DECLARATION

Declaration made this........day of........................(Month, year).
I, ...(NAME), being of sound mind, willfully and
voluntarily make known my desire that my dying shall not be artificially
prolonged under the circumstances set forth below, do hereby declare:

If at any time I should have an incurable injury, disease, or illness
certified to be a terminal condition by 2 physicians who have personally
examined me, one of whom shall be my attending physician, and the physicians
have determined that my death will occur whether or not life-sustaining
procedures are utilized and where the application of life-sustaining procedures
would serve only to artificially prolong the dying process, I direct that such
procedures be withheld or withdrawn, and that I be permitted to die naturally
with only the administration of medication, sustenance, or the performance of
any medical procedure deemed necessary to provide me with comfort care.

In the absence of my ability to give directions regarding the use of such
life-sustaining procedures, it is my intention that this declaration shall be
honored by my family and physicians as the final expression of my right to
refuse medical or surgical treatment and accept the consequences of such
refusal.

I understand the full import of this declaration, and I am emotionally and
mentally competent to make this declaration.

Signed.......................................

State of.........................
...........................County

We, the declarant and witnesses, being duly sworn each declare to the notary
public or justice of the peace or other official signing below as follows:

1. The declarant signed the instrument as a free and voluntary act for the
purposes expressed, or expressly directed another to sign for him.

2. Each witness signed at the request of the declarant, in his presence,
and in the presence of the other witness.

3. To the best of my knowledge, at the time of the signing the declarant
was at least 18 years of age, and was of sane mind and under no constraint or
undue influence.

...................................Declarant
....................................Witness
....................................Witness

The affidavit shall be made before a notary public or justice of the peace
or other official authorized to administer oaths in the place of execution, who
shall not also serve as a witness, and who shall complete and sign a certificate in content and form substantially as follows:

Sworn to me and signed before me by ...., declarant
.... and ...., witnesses
on ....
....
Signature
....
Official Capacity

STATE OF NORTH CAROLINA

"DECLARATION OF A DESIRE FOR A NATURAL DEATH"

"I, ...(NAME), being of sound mind, desire that my life not be prolonged by extraordinary means if my condition is determined to be terminal and incurable. I am aware and understand that this writing authorizes a physician to withhold or discontinue extraordinary means.

"This the........day of...
                    Signature...

"I hereby state that the declarant, ..., being of sound mind signed the above declaration in my presence and that I am not related to the declarant by blood or marriage and that I do not know or have a reasonable expectation that I would be entitled to any portion of the estate of the declarant under any existing will or codicil of the declarant or as an heir under the Intestate Succession Act if the declarant died on this date without a will. I also state that I am not the declarant's attending physician or an employee of the declarant's attending physician, or an employee of a health facility in which the declarant is a patient or an employee of a nursing home or any group-care home where the declarant resides. I further state that I do not now have any claim against the declarant.

                    Witness......................................
                    Witness......................................"

The clerk or the assistant clerk, or a notary public may, upon proper proof, certify the declaration as follows:

"CERTIFICATE"

"I, ..., Clerk (Assistant Clerk) of Superior Court or Notary Public (circle one as appropriate) for .... County hereby certify that ...., the declarant , appeared before me and swore to me and to the witnesses in my presence that this instrument is his Declaration Of A Desire For A Natural Death, and that he had willingly and voluntarily made and executed it as his free act and deed for the purposes expressed in it.

"I further certify that .... and ...., witnesses, appeared before me and swore that they witnessed ...., declarant, sign the attached declaration, believing him to be of sound mind; and also swore that at the time they witnessed the declaration (i) they were not related within the third degree to the declarant or to the declarant's spouse, and (ii) they did not know or have a reasonable expectation that they would be entitled to any portion of the estate of the declarant upon the declarant's eath under any will of the declarant or codicil thereto then existing or under the Intestate Succession Act as it provides at that time, and (iii) they were not a physician attending the declarant or an employee of an attending physician or an employee of a health facility in which the declarant was a patient or an employee of a nursing home or any group-care home in which the declarant resided, and (iv) they did not have a claim against the declarant. I further certify that I am satisfied as to the genuineness and due execution of the declaration.

"This the........day of ....
Clerk (Assistant Clerk) of Superior Court or Notary Public
(circle one as appropriate) for the County of ...."

STATE OF NORTH CAROLINA

If the testimony of one or both of the witnesses is not available the clerk or the assistant clerk, or a notary public or superior court may, upon proper proof, certify the declaration as follows:

"CERTIFICATE"

"I, ..., Clerk (Assistant Clerk) of Court for the Superior Court or Notary Public (circle one as appropriate) of............... County hereby certify that based upon the evidence before me I am satisfied as to the genuineness and due execution of the attached declaration by ...., declarant, and that the declarant's signature was witnessed by .... and ...., who at the time of the declaration met the qualifications of G.S.90-321(c)(3).
    "This the........day of............., ...
                              ....
                              Clerk (Assistant Clerk) of Superior Court
                              or Notary Public (circle one as appropriate)
                              for ....County."

STATE OF OKLAHOMA

DIRECTIVE TO PHYSICIANS

Directive made this........day of.........................(Month, year).
I, ...(NAME), being of sound mind and twenty-one
(21) years of age or older, willfully and voluntarily make known my desire that
my life shall not be artificially prolonged under the circumstances set forth
below, and do hereby declare:

1. If at any time I should have an incurable irreversible condition
caused by injury, disease, or illness certified to be a terminal condition
by two physicians, I direct that life-sustaining procedures be withheld or
withdrawn and that I be permitted to die naturally, if the application of
life-sustaining procedures would serve only to artificially prolong the moment
of my death and my attending physician determines that my death is imminent
whether or not life-sustaining procedures are utilized;

2. In the absence of my ability to give directions regarding the use of
such life-sustaining procedures, it is my intention that this directive shall
be honored by my family and physicians as the final expression of my legal
right to refuse medical or surgical treatment and accept the consequences of
such refusal;

3. If I have been diagnosed as pregnant and that diagnosis is known to my
physician, this directive shall have no force or effect during the course of
my pregnancy;

4. I have been diagnosed and notified as having a terminal condition by
................................, M.D. or D.O., whose address is ....
................................, and whose telephone number is ....
I understand that if I have not filled in the name and address of the physician, it shall be presumed that I did not have a terminal condition when I made
out this directive;

5. This directive shall be in effect until it is revoked;

6. I understand the full import of this directive and I am emotionally
and mentally competent to make this directive;

7. I understand that I may revoke this directive at any time.

Signed....................................

City, County, and State of Residence..

The declarant has been personally known to me and I believe said declarant
to be of sound mind. I am twenty-one (21) years of age or older, I am not
related to the declarant by blood or marriage, nor would I be entitled to any
portion of the estate of the declarant upon the death of said declarant, nor am
I the attending physician of the declarant or an employee of the attending

physician or a health care facility in which the declarant is a patient, or a patient in the health care facility in which the declarant is a patient, nor am I financially responsible for the medical care of the declarant, or any person who has a claim against any portion of the estate of the declarant upon the death of the declarant.

Witness...................................

Witness...................................

State of Oklahoma
County of......................
 Before me, the undersigned authority, on this day personally appeared .... (Declarant), ... (Witness) and .... (Witness) whose names are subscribed to the foregoing instrument in their respective capacities, and, all of said persons being by me duly sworn, the declarant declared to me and to the said witnesses in my presence that said instrument is his or her "Directive to Physicians," and that the declarant had willingly and voluntarily made and executed it as the free act and deed of the declarant for the purposes therein expressed.

 The foregoing instrument was acknowledged before me this........day of ...., 19......

Signed...................................
Notary Public in and for
.... County, Oklahoma

My Commission Expires ....day of...................., 19.......

STATE OF OREGON

DIRECTIVE TO PHYSICIANS

Directive made this........day of ....(Month, year).
I, ..., being of sound mind, wilfully and
voluntarily make known my desire that my life shall not be artificially
prolonged under the circumstances set forth below and do hereby declare:

1. If at any time I should have an incurable injury, disease or illness
certified to be a terminal condition by two physicians, one of whom is the
attending physician, and where the application of life-sustaining procedures
would serve only to artificially prolong the moment of my death and where my
physician determines that my death is imminent whether or not life-sustaining
procedures are utilized, I direct that such procedures be withheld or withdrawn, and that I be permitted to die naturally.

2. In the absence of my ability to give directions regarding the use of
such life-sustaining procedures, it is my intention that this directive shall
be honored by my family and physician(s) as the final expression of my legal
right to refuse medical or surgical treatment and accept the consequences from
such refusal.

3. I understand the full import of this directive and I am emotionally and
mentally competent to make this directive.

            Signed...

            City, County, and State of Residence.......................

I hereby witness this directive and attest that:

(1) I personally know the Declarant and believe the Declarant to be of
sound mind.

(2) To the best of my knowledge, at the time of the execution of this
directive, I:
    (a) Am not related to the Declarant by blood or marriage,
    (b) Do not have any claim on the estate of the Declarant,
    (c) Am not entitled to any portion of the Declarant's estate by any will
or by operation of law, and
    (d) Am not a physician attending the Declarant, a person employed by a
physician attending the Declarant or a person employed by a health facility in
which the Declarant is a patient.

(3) I understand that if I have not witnessed this directive in good faith
I may be responsible for any damages that arise out of giving this directive
its intended effect.

            Witness...

            Witness...

STATE OF SOUTH CAROLINA

DECLARATION OF A DESIRE FOR A NATURAL DEATH

COUNTY OF ....

    I, ...(NAME), a resident of and domiciled in the City of ...., County of ....,
State of South Carolina, make this Declaration this........day of ....,
19......

    I wilfully and voluntarily make known my desire that no life-sustaining procedures be used to prolong my dying if my condition is terminal, and I do hereby declare:

    If at any time I have an incurable injury, disease, or illness certified to be a terminal condition by two physicians who have personally examined me, one of whom is my attending physician, and the physicians have determined that my death will occur without the use of life-sustaining procedures and where the application of life-sustaining procedures would serve only to prolong the dying process, I direct that such procedures be withheld or withdrawn, and that I be permitted to die naturally with only the administration of medication or the performance of any medical procedure necessary to provide me with comfort care.

    In the absence of my ability to give directions regarding the use of such life-sustaining procedures, it is my intention that this Declaration be honored by my family and physicians as the final expression of my legal right to refuse medical or surgical treatment and I accept the consequences from such refusal.

    I am aware that this Declaration authorizes a physician to withhold or withdraw life-sustaining procedures. I am emotionally and mentally competent to make this Declaration.

    THIS DECLARATION MAY BE REVOKED BY THE DECLARANT, WITHOUT REGARD TO HIS PHYSICAL OR MENTAL CONDITION.

    (1) BY BEING DEFACED, TORN, OBLITERATED, OR OTHERWISE DESTROYED BY THE DECLARANT OR BY SOME PERSON IN THE PRESENCE OF AND BY THE DIRECTION OF THE DECLARANT.

    (2) BY A WRITTEN REVOCATION SIGNED AND DATED BY THE DECLARANT EXPRESSING HIS OR HER INTENT TO REVOKE. THE REVOCATION SHALL BECOME EFFECTIVE ONLY UPON COMMUNICATION TO THE ATTENDING PHYSICIAN BY THE DECLARANT OR BY A PERSON ACTING ON BEHALF OF THE DECLARANT. THE ATTENDING PHYSICIAN SHALL RECORD IN THE PATIENT'S MEDICAL RECORD THE TIME AND DATE WHEN HE RECEIVED NOTIFICATION OF THE WRITTEN REVOCATION.

    (3) BY A VERBAL EXPRESSION BY THE DECLARANT OF HIS INTENT TO REVOKE THE DECLARATION. THE REVOCATION SHALL BECOME EFFECTIVE ONLY UPON COMMUNICATION TO THE ATTENDING PHYSICIAN BY THE DECLARANT. THE ATTENDING PHYSICIAN SHALL RECORD IN THE PATIENT'S MEDICAL RECORD THE TIME, DATE, AND PLACE OF THE REVOCATION AND THE TIME, DATE, AND PLACE, IF DIFFERENT, OF WHEN HE RECEIVED NOTIFICATION OF THE REVOCATION.

    ....
    Declarant

STATE OF ....   AFFIDAVIT
COUNTY OF ....
    We, ..., ..., and
..................................., the witnesses whose names are signed to the foregoing Declaration, dated the........day of ...., 19....,
being first duly sworn, do hereby declare to the undersigned authority that the

Declaration was on that date signed by the said declarant as and for his
DECLARATION OF A DESIRE FOR A NATURAL DEATH in our presence and we, at his
request and in his presence, and in the presence of each other, did thereunto
subscribe our names as witnesses on that date. The declarant is personally
known to us and we believe him to be of sound mind. None of us is disqualified
as a witness to this Declaration by any provision of the South Carolina Death
With Dignity Act. None of us is related to the declarant by blood or marriage;
nor directly financially responsible for the declarant's medical care; nor
entitled to any portion of the declarant's estate upon his decease, whether
under any will or as an heir by intestate succession; nor the beneficiary of a
life insurance policy of the declarant; nor the declarant's attending physician; nor an employee of such attending physician; nor a person who has a claim
against the declarant's decedent's estate as of this time. No more than one of
us is an employee of a health facility in which the declarant is a patient. If
the declarant is a patient in a hospital or skilled or intermediate care
nursing facility at the date of execution of this Declaration at least one of
us is an ombudsman designated by the State Ombudsman, Office of the Governor.

....
Witness
....
Witness
....
Witness

Subscribed, sworn to, and acknowledged before me by ....,
the declarant, and subscribed and sworn to before me by ....,
..................................., and ....,
the witnesses, this........day of ...., 19....

....
Notary Public for
My commission expires: ....

SEAL

STATE OF TENNESSEE

LIVING WILL

I, ...(NAME), willfully and voluntarily make known my desire that my dying shall not be artificially prolonged under the circumstances set forth below, and do hereby declare:

If at any time I should have a terminal condition and my attending physician has determined that there can be no recovery from such condition and my death is imminent, where the application of life-prolonging procedures would serve only to artificially prolong the dying process, I direct that such procedures be withheld or withdrawn, and that I be permitted to die naturally with only the administration of medications or the performance of any medical procedure deemed necessary to provide me with comfortable care or to alleviate pain.

In the absence of my ability to give directions regarding the use of such life-prolonging procedures, it is my intention that this declaration shall be honored by my family and physician as the final expression of my legal right to refuse medical or surgical treatment and accept the consequences of such refusal.

I understand the full import of this declaration, and I am emotionally and mentally competent to make this declaration. In acknowledgment whereof, I do hereinafter affix my signature on this the........day of ...., 19....

....
Declarant

We, the subscribing witnesses hereto, are personally acquainted with and subscribe our names hereto at the request of the declarant, an adult, whom we believe to be of sound mind, fully aware of the action taken herein and its possible consequence.

We, the undersigned witnesses, further declare that we are not related to the declarant by blood or marriage; that we are not entitled to any portion of the estate of the declarant upon his decease under any will or codicil thereto presently existing or by operation of law then existing; that we are not the attending physician, an employee of the attending physician or a health facility in which the declarant is a patient; and that we are not a person who, at the present time, has a claim against any portion of the estate of the declarant upon his death.

....
Witness
....
Witness

Subscribed, sworn to, and acknowledged before me by....................., the declarant, and subscribed and sworn to before me by...................... and ...., witnesses, this........day of ...., 19......

....
Notary Public

STATE OF TEXAS

"DIRECTIVE TO PHYSICIANS

"Directive made this.......day of ....(Month, year).
"I ...., being of sound mind, willfully and
voluntarily make known my desire that my life shall not be artificially
prolonged under the circumstances set forth below, and do hereby declare:
    "1. If at any time I should have an incurable condition caused by injury,
disease, or illness certified to be a terminal condition by two physicians, and
where the application of life-sustaining procedures would serve only to
artificially prolong the moment of my death and where my attending physician
determines that my death is imminent whether or not life-sustaining procedures
are utilized, I direct that such procedures be withheld or withdrawn, and that
I be permitted to die naturally.
    "2. In the absence of my ability to give directions regarding the use of
such life-sustaining procedures, it is my intention that this directive shall
be honored by my family and physicians as the final expression of my legal
right to refuse medical or surgical treatment and accept the consequences from
such refusal.
    "3. If I have been diagnosed as pregnant and that diagnosis is known to my
physician, this directive shall have no force or effect during the course of my
pregnancy.
    "4. I have been diagnosed and notified as having a terminal condition by
........................., M.D. or D.O., whose address is ....
...., and whose telephone number
is .... I understand that if I have not filled in the
physician's name and address, it shall be presumed that I did not have a
terminal condition when I made out this directive.
    "5. This directive shall be in effect until it is revoked.
    "6. I understand the full import of this directive and I am emotionally
and mentally competent to make this directive.
    "7. I understand that I may revoke this directive at any time.

                    "Signed ....

City, County, and State of Residence..

The declarant has been personally known to me and I believe him or her to be of
sound mind. I am not related to the declarant by blood or marriage, nor would
I be entitled to any portion of the declarant's estate on his decease, nor am I
the attending physician of declarant or an employee of the attending physician
or a health facility in which declarant is a patient, or any person who has a
claim against any portion of the estate of the declarant upon his decease.

                    "Witness ....

                    "Witness ...."

STATE OF UTAH

DIRECTIVE TO PHYSICIANS AND PROVIDERS OF MEDICAL SERVICES
(Pursuant to Section 75-2-1104, UCA)

This directive is made this........day of ...., ...

1. I, ...(NAME), being of sound mind, willfully and voluntarily make known my desire that my life not be artificially prolonged by life-sustaining procedures except as I may otherwise provide in this directive.

2. I declare that if at any time I should have an injury, disease, or illness, which is certified in writing to be a terminal condition by two physicians who have personally examined me, and in the opinion of those physicians the application of life-sustaining procedures would serve only to unnaturally prolong the moment of my death and to unnaturally postpone or prolong the dying process, I direct that these procedures be withheld or withdrawn and my death be permitted to occur naturally.

3. I expressly intend this directive to be a final expression of my legal right to refuse medical or surgical treatment and to accept the consequences from this refusal which shall remain in effect notwithstanding my future inability to give current medical directions to treating physicians and other providers of medical services.

4. I understand that the term "life-sustaining procedure" does not include the administration of medication or sustenance, or the performance of any medical procedure deemed necessary to provide comfort care, or to alleviate pain, except to the extent I specify below that any of these procedures be considered life-sustaining:
....

5. I reserve the right to give current medical directions to physicians and other providers of medical services so long as I am able, even though these directions may conflict with the above written directive that life-sustaining procedures be withheld or withdrawn.

6. I understand the full import of this directive and declare that I am emotionally and mentally competent to make this directive.

.....................................Declarant's signature

....
City, County, and State of Residence

We witnesses certify that each of us is 18 years of age or older and each personally witnessed the declarant sign or direct the signing of this directive; that we are acquainted with the declarant and believe him to be of sound mind; that the declarant's desires are as expressed above; that neither of us is a person who signed the above directive on behalf of the declarant; that we are not related to the declarant by blood or marriage nor are we entitled to any portion of declarant's estate according to the laws of intestate succession of this state or under any will or codicil of declarant; that we are not directly financially responsible for declarant's medical care; and that we are not agents of any health care facility in which the declarant may be a patient at the time of signing this directive.

....
Signature of Witness   Signature of Witness

....
Address of Witness   Address of Witness

STATE OF UTAH

DIRECTIVE TO PHYSICIANS AND PROVIDERS OF MEDICAL SERVICES
AFTER INJURY OR ILLNESS IS INCURRED
(Pursuant to Section 75-2-1105, UCA)

I, ..., certify that I am serving as the attending physician for .... of ...., who has been under my care since the........day of ...., ...

1. This declarant ...., is currently suffering from the following injury, disease, or illness:
....
....
....

2. I certify that I have explained to the declarant to the extent he is able to understand, and to the available persons acting as proxy, the reasonable available alternatives for his care and treatment.

3. I certify that the care and treatment alternatives directed below are:
.... (a) directed by the declarant; or
.... (b) that the declarant has a physical or medical condition which renders him unable to give personal directions for care and treatment and that the care and treatment alternatives directed below are in my opinion, and in the opinion of the declarant's proxy, what the declarant would probably decide if able to give current directions concerning his care and treatment.

Date: ....
                                 Signature of attending physician

The following care and treatment or withholding of treatment is directed with respect to the declarant:
....
....
....
....

Relationship to declarant   ....
 of person signing on   Signature of declarant or person
   declarant's behalf,   authorized by law to sign
     if applicable.   directive as a proxy on
                                    behalf of declarant

                                 ....
                                 Address of Signer
                                 ....
                                 City, County, and State of
                                    residence of Signer

We witnesses certify that each of us is 18 years of age or older; that we personally witnessed the declarant or a proxy sign this directive; that we are acquainted with the declarant and, if the foregoing was signed by a proxy, also the proxy; that we believe that care and treatment alternatives directed above are in the interest of declarant and what declarant has decided or would probably decide for himself if able to give current directions concerning his care and treatment; that neither of us signed the above directive for or on behalf of declarant; that we are not related to the declarant by blood or marriage nor are we entitled to any portion of declarant's estate according to the laws of intestate succession of this state or under any will or codicil of the declarant; that we are not directly financially responsible for declarant's medical care; and that we are not agents of any health care facility in which declarant may be a patient at the time of signing this directive.

....
Signature of Witness   Signature of Witness

....
Address of Witness   Address of Witness

****

UTAH SPECIAL POWER OF ATTORNEY

I, ..., of ...., this........day of ...., ..., being of sound mind, willfully and voluntarily appoint ...., of .... as my agent and attorney-in-fact, without substitution, with lawful authority to execute a directive on my behalf under Section 75-2-1105, governing the care and treatment to be administered to or withheld from me at any time after I incur an injury, disease, or illness which renders me unable to give current directions to attending physicians and other providers of medical services.

I understand that "life-sustaining procedures" do not include the administration of medication or sustenance, or the performance of any medical procedure deemed necessary to provide comfort care, or to alleviate pain, unless my attorney-in-fact specifies these procedures be considered life-sustaining.

I have carefully selected my above-named agent with confidence in the belief that this person's familiarity with my desires, beliefs, and attitudes will result in directions to attending physicians and providers of medical services which would probably be the same as I would give if able to do so.

This power of attorney shall be and remain in effect from the time my attending physician certifies that I have incurred a physical or mental condition rendering me unable to give current directions to attending physicians and other providers of medical services as to my care and treatment.

....
Signature of Principal

STATE OF ....)
                         : ss.
County of ....)

On the........day of ...., ..., personally appeared before me ...., who duly acknowledged to me that he has read and fully understands the foregoing power of attorney, executed the same of his own volition and for the purposes set forth, and that he was acting under no constraint or undue influence whatsoever.

....
Notary Public

My commission expires:
Residing at: ....
....

STATE OF VERMONT

TERMINAL CARE DOCUMENT

"To my family, my physician, my lawyer, my clergyman. To any medical facility in whose care I happen to be. To any individual who may become responsible for my health, welfare, or affairs.

"Death is as much a reality as birth, growth, maturity, and old age--it is the one certainty of life. If the time comes when I, ..., can no longer take part in decisions of my own future, let this statement stand as an expression of my wishes, while I am still of sound mind.

"If the situation should arise in which I am in a terminal state and there is no reasonable expectation of my recovery, I direct that I be allowed to die a natural death and that my life not be prolonged by extraordinary measures. I do, however, ask that medication be mercifully administered to me to alleviate suffering even though this may shorten my remaining life.

"This statement is made after careful consideration and is in accordance with my strong convictions and beliefs. I want the wishes and directions here expressed carried out to the extent permitted by law. Insofar as they are not legally enforceable, I hope that those to whom this will is addressed will regard themselves as morally bound by these provisions.

Signed: ....

Date:...

Witness: ....

Witness: ....

Copies of this request have been given to:

....

....

...."

STATE OF VIRGINIA

DECLARATION

Declaration made this........day of ....(Month, year).

I, ...(NAME), willfully and voluntarily make known my desire that my dying shall not be artificially prolonged under the circumstances set forth below, and do hereby declare:

If at any time I should have a terminal condition and my attending physician has determined that there can be no recovery from such condition and my death is imminent, where the application of life-prolonging procedures would serve only to artificially prolong the dying process, I direct that such procedures be withheld or withdrawn, and that I be permitted to die naturally with only the administration of medication or the performance of any medical procedure deemed necessary to provide me with comfort care or to alleviate pain.

In the absence of my ability to give directions regarding the use of such life-prolonging procedures, it is my intention that this declaration shall be honored by my family and physician as the final expression of my legal right to refuse medical or surgical treatment and accept the consequences of such refusal.

I understand the full import of this declaration and I am emotionally and mentally competent to make this declaration...............................
                                   (Signed)

The declarant is known to me and I believe him or her to be of sound mind.

.................................Witness ....Witness

STATE OF WASHINGTON

DIRECTIVE TO PHYSICIANS

Directive made this........day of ....(Month, year).

I, ...(NAME), being of sound mind, wilfully and voluntarily make known my desire that my life shall not be artificially prolonged under the circumstances set forth below, and do hereby declare that:

(a) If at any time I should have an incurable injury, disease, or illness certified to be a terminal condition by two physicians, and where the application of life-sustaining procedures would serve only to artificially prolong the moment of my death and where my physician determines that my death is imminent whether or not life-sustaining procedures are utilized, I direct that such procedures be withheld or withdrawn, and that I be permitted to die naturally.

(b) In the absence of my ability to give directions regarding the use of such life-sustaining procedures, it is my intention that this directive shall be honored by my family and physician(s) as the final expression of my legal right to refuse medical or surgical treatment and I accept the consequences from such refusal.

(c) If I have been diagnosed as pregnant and that diagnosis is known to my physician, this directive shall have no force or effect during the course of my pregnancy.

(d) I understand the full import of this directive and I am emotionally and mentally competent to make this directive.

Signed ....
City, County, and State of Residence...

The declarer has been personally known to me and I believe him or her to be of sound mind.

Witness ....

Witness ....

(Prior to effectuating a directive the diagnosis of a terminal condition by two physicians shall be verified in writing, attached to the directive, and made a permanent part of the patient's medical records.)

STATE OF WEST VIRGINIA

"DECLARATION

"Declaration made this........day of ....(Month, year).
I, ...(NAME), being of sound mind, willfully and
voluntarily make known my desires that my dying shall not be artificially
prolonged under the circumstances set forth below, do declare:

"If at any time I should have an incurable injury, disease, or illness
certified to be a terminal condition by two physicians who have personally
examined me, one of whom is my attending physician, and the physicians have
determined that my death will occur whether or not life-sustaining procedures
are utilized and where the application of life-sustaining procedures would
serve only to artificially prolong the dying process, I direct that such
procedures be withheld or withdrawn, and that I be permitted to die naturally
with only the administration of nutrition, medication, or the performance of
any medical procedure deemed necessary to provide me with comfort, care, or to
alleviate pain.

"In the absence of my ability to give directions regarding the use of such
life-sustaining procedures, it is my intention that this declaration be honored
by my family and physician(s) as the final expression of my legal right to
refuse medical or surgical treatment and accept the consequences resulting from
such refusal.

"I understand the full import of this declaration and I am emotionally and
mentally competent to make this declaration.

"Signed ....

"Address ....

....

"I did not sign the declarant's signature above for or at the direction of
the declarant. I am at least eighteen years of age and am not related to the
declarant by blood or marriage, entitled to any portion of the estate of the
declarant according to the laws of intestate succession of the State of West
Virginia or to the best of my knowledge under any will of declarant or codicil
thereto, or directly financially responsible for declarant's medical care. I
am not the declarant's attending physician, an employee of the attending
physician, nor an employee of the health facility in which the declarant is a
patient.

"Witness ....

"Witness ....

"STATE OF ....,

"COUNTY OF ...., to-wit:
"This day personally appeared before me, the undersigned authority, a

Notary Public in and for .... County, ... (State), ... (witness) and .... (witness) who, being first duly sworn, say that they are the subscribing witnesses to the declaration of .... (declarant), which declaration is dated the.......day of ...., 19, ...; and that on the said date the said .... (declarant), the declarant, signed, sealed, published, and declared the same as and for his declaration, in the presence of both these affiants; and that these affiants, at the request of said declarant, in the presence of each other, and in the presence of said declarant, all present at the same time, signed their names as attesting witnesses to said declaration.

   "Affiants further say that this affidavit is made at the request of...... .... (declarant), declarant, and in his presence, and that .... (declarant), at the time the declaration was execu-ted, was in the opinion of affiants, of sound mind and memory, and over the age of eighteen years.

   ....

   ....

   "Taken, subscribed, and sworn to before me by .... (witness) and .... (witness) this........day of ...., 19.......
   "My commission expires:
                     "..
                           Notary Public."

STATE OF WISCONSIN

DECLARATION TO PHYSICIANS

Declaration made this........day of ....(month),........(year).

1. I, ..., being of sound mind, wilfully and voluntarily state my desire that my dying may not be artificially prolonged if I have an incurable injury or illness certified to be a terminal condition by 2 physicians who have personally examined me, one of whom is my attending physician, and if the physicians have determined that my death is imminent whether or not life-sustaining procedures are utilized because the application of life-sustaining procedures would serve only to prolong artificially the dying process. Under these circumstances, I direct that life-sustaining procedures be withheld or withdrawn and that I be permitted to die naturally, with only the continuation of nutritional support and the alleviation of pain by administering medication or other medical procedure.

2. If I am unable to give directions regarding the use of life-sustaining procedures, I intend that my family and physician honor this declaration as the final expression of my legal right to refuse medical or surgical treatment and to accept the consequences from this refusal.

3. If I have been diagnosed as pregnant and my physician knows of this diagnosis, this declaration has no effect during the course of my pregnancy.

4. This declaration takes effect immediately.

I understand this declaration and I am emotionally and mentally competent to make this declaration.

Signed..

Address..

I know the declarant personally and I believe him or her to be of sound mind. I am not related to the declarant by blood or marriage, and am not entitled to any portion of the declarant's estate under any will of the declarant. I am neither the declarant's attending physician nor attending nurse nor an employee of the attending physician or of the inpatient health care facility in which the declarant may be a patient and I have no claim against the declarant's estate at this time.

Witness..

Witness..

STATE OF WYOMING

DECLARATION

Declaration made this........day of ....(Month, year).
I, ...(NAME), being of sound mind, willfully and
voluntarily make known my desire that my dying shall not be artificially
prolonged under the circumstances set forth below, do hereby declare:

If at any time I should have an incurable injury, disease, or other
illness certified to be a terminal condition by two (2) physicians who have
personally examined me, one (1) of whom shall be my attending physician, and
the physicians have determined that my death will occur whether or not
life-sustaining procedures are utilized and where the application of life-sustaining procedures would serve only to artificially prolong the dying process,
I direct that such procedures be withheld or withdrawn, and that I be permitted
to die naturally with only the administration of medication or the performance
of any medical procedure deemed necessary to provide me with comfort care.

If, in spite of this declaration, I am comatose or otherwise unable to
make treatment decisions for myself, I HEREBY designate ....
to make treatment decisions for me.

In the absence of my ability to give directions regarding the use of
life-sustaining procedures, it is my intention that this declaration shall be
honored by my family and physician(s) and agent as the final expression of my
legal right to refuse medical or surgical treatment and accept the consequences
from this refusal. I understand the full import of this declaration and I am
emotionally and mentally competent to make this declaration.

Signed...

City, County, and State of Residence..................................

The declarant has been personally known to me and I believe him or her to
be of sound mind. I did not sign the declarant's signature above for or at the
direction of the declarant. I am not related to the declarant by blood or
marriage, entitled to any portion of the estate of the declarant according to
the laws of intestate succession or under any will of the declarant or codicil
thereto, or directly financially responsible for declarant's medical care.

Witness..

Witness..

APPENDIX B

INSTRUCTIONS AND FORM TO EXECUTE A LIVING WILL IN STATES WITHOUT
SPECIFIC NATURAL DEATH LAWS

(a) Fill in your name in the blank in paragraph 2.

(b) Under "Optional specific provisions," add any personalized instructions you desire. For example: "I freely give my permission for donations of any of my tissues or organs which would be of value as transplants." "Measures of artificial life-support in the face of imminent death which I specifically refuse are: (1) Nasogastric tube feeding when I am paralyzed or unable to take nourishment by mouth; (2) amputation of any of my limbs; (3) blood transfusions or dialysis; (4) mechanical respiration when I am no longer able to breathe on my own; (5) cardio-pulmonary resuscitation by any means when my heart has stopped beating; or _____." "I wish to live out my last days at home rather than in a hospital if it does not jeopardize the chance of my recovery to a meaningful and sentient life and does not impose an undue burden on my family."

(c) If you wish to designate someone else to make medical treatment decisions on your behalf in the event you become incompetent or otherwise incapacitated, fill in the optional Durable Power of Attorney section. Indicate the name of the individual you designate as your proxy in the space provided (after first discussing this matter with the person in question).

(d) Date the Living Will document and sign your name in the appropriate spaces. Under your signature, print or type your full name and address. Two witnesses to this document must sign on the lines indicated and their full names and addresses are to be printed or typed under their signatures.

(e) On the second page of the Living Will document is an optional notarization form. If you choose to fill out the Durable Power of Attorney, you must have the Living Will notarized. It is highly recommended in any case that your have the Will notarized to indicate the seriousness of your intent.

(f) Finally, spaces are provided for the names and addresses of individuals to whom you have given copies of your Living Will.

LIVING WILL

To my Family, my Physician, my Lawyer, my Clergyman. To any Medical Facility in whose care I happen to be. To any individual who may become responsible for my health, welfare, or affairs.

Death is as much a reality as birth, growth, maturity, and old age--it is the one certainty of life. If the time comes when I, _____ _____(NAME), can no longer take part in decisions for my own future, let this statement stand as an expression of my wishes and directions while I am still of sound mind.

If a situation should arise when I am in a terminal state in which there is no reasonable expectation of my recovery from extreme physical or mental disability, I direct that I be allowed to die and not be kept alive by medications, artificial means, or "heroic" or extraordinary measures. I do, however, ask that medication be mercifully administered to me to alleviate suffering even though this may shorten my remaining life.

This statement is made after careful consideration and is in accordance with my strong convictions and beliefs. I want the wishes and directions here expressed carried out to the extent permitted by law. To the extent that the provisions of this Living Will are not legally enforceable, I hope that those to whom this Will is addressed will regard themselves as morally bound by them.

Optional specific provisions:

DURABLE POWER OF ATTORNEY (optional)

I hereby designate _____ to serve as my attorney-in-fact for the purpose of making medical treatment decisions. This power of attorney shall remain effective in the event that I become incompetent or otherwise unable to make such decisions for myself.

Dated_____   Signature_____

Witness_____   _____

_____
                               Below signature, print or type full
_____   name and address of person signing

Witness_____

_____

_____
Below signatures of witnesses,
print or type their full names
and addresses

Optional Notarization:

STATE OF
COUNTY OF

"Sworn and subscribed to before me this _____ day of _____, 19____."

_____
Notary Public

(SEAL)

Copies of this Will have been given to the following:

Name   _____
Address _____
           _____

Name   _____
Address _____
           _____

Name   _____
Address _____
           _____